Tell Me About
The Human Body

Tell Me About
The Human Body

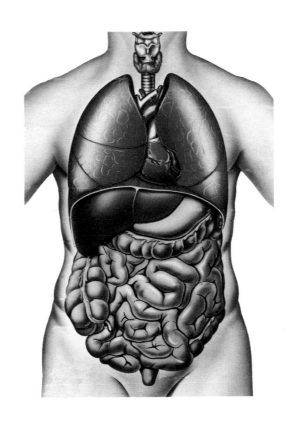

WATERBIRD BOOKS

Columbus, Ohio

This edition published in the United States of America in 2004 by
Waterbird Books
an imprint of McGraw-Hill Children's Publishing,
a Division of The McGraw-Hill Companies
8720 Orion Place
Columbus, Ohio 43240-2111

www.MHkids.com

Library of Congress Cataloging-in-Publication Data is on file with the publisher.

Printed in China

ISBN 0-7696-3380-3

1 2 3 4 5 6 7 8 9 10 TOP 09 08 07 06 05 04

CONTENTS

THE SENSES 6

BONES AND MUSCLES 32

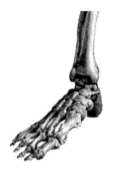

HEART AND CIRCULATION 62

ORGANS AND DIGESTION 80

BRAIN AND NERVOUS SYSTEM 116

GENETICS AND REPRODUCTION 138

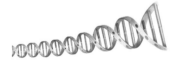

GENERAL KNOWLEDGE 160

ANIMAL PHYSIOLOGY 196

THE
SENSES

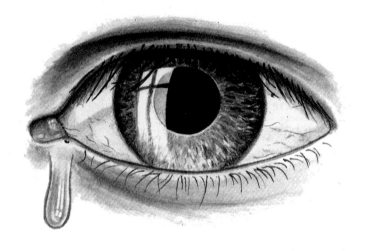

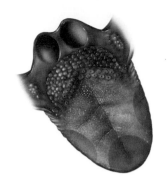

CONTENTS

WHAT PURPOSE DO TEARS SERVE? 8
HOW DO DEAF PEOPLE COMMUNICATE? 9

WHAT IS BODY LANGUAGE? 10
HOW SENSITIVE IS HEARING? 11

HOW SIMILAR ARE TASTE AND SMELL? 12
HOW DO WE SMELL? 13

HOW DO WE RECOGNIZE A SPECIFIC TASTE? 14
WHEN DO WE LOSE OUR SENSE OF TASTE? 15

HOW IS THE EYE MADE? 16
HOW DO WE SEE IN COLOR? 17

WHAT IS THE RETINA? 18
WHAT MAKES THE EYEBALL MOVE? 19

WHAT IS PUPIL REFLEX? 20
WHAT IS THE FOCUSING MECHANISM IN THE EYE? 21

WHAT ARE THE PARTS OF THE EAR? 22
WHAT IS THE COCHLEA? 23

WHEN DO WE SEE IMAGES UPSIDE DOWN? 24
WHAT ARE CONTACT LENSES? 25

WHAT IS SKIN? 26
WHAT IS SENSATION? 27

WHY IS TOUCH AN IMPORTANT SENSE? 28
WHY ARE SOME BODY PARTS MORE SENSITIVE THAN OTHERS? 29

WHY DO ONIONS MAKE YOU CRY? 30
WHAT IS AN OPTICAL ILLUSION? 31

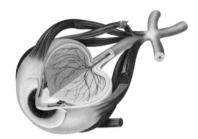

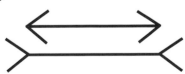

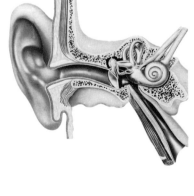

WHAT PURPOSE DO TEARS SERVE?

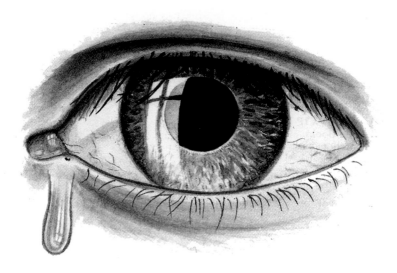

Part of the essential protection of the eyes, tears bathe the outer layer of the eyeball, called the *cornea*, and keep it clear of foreign particles. Tears prevent the cornea from drying out, which would otherwise result in blindness. Tears are actually a secretion of the lacrimal glands, which lie behind each eyelid. When the eyelid blinks, a small amount of fluid is sucked from the glands and secreted through small ducts in the underside of the lid. Some emotions, such as grief and sadness, can cause the muscles around the lacrimal glands to tighten up, forcing out the tear fluid. Two lacrimal ducts at the inner corner of each eye then allow the tears to flow out, after they have passed across the eyeball.

FACT FILE

Lacrimal fluid is mainly a salt solution. It also contains anti-bacterial elements and proteins that protect against infection.

HOW DO DEAF PEOPLE COMMUNICATE?

There are two main ways in which deaf or hearing-impaired people communicate–speech reading and sign language.

Popularly known as reading lips, speech reading is where a person can understand what another person is saying by watching the movements of the speaker's mouth, along with those of the face and body.

Sign language is how people "talk" with their hands and usually consists of two elements, finger spelling and actual sign language. Finger spelling has a different hand signal for each letter of the alphabet. Sign language has gestures that stand for objects and ideas. Sign language allows deaf people to communicate with other individuals who understand finger spelling and sign language.

FACT FILE

Although deafness poses special challenges, the condition does not hinder achievement in a wide variety of occupations. The German composer Ludwig van Beethoven wrote some of his finest music after he became deaf.

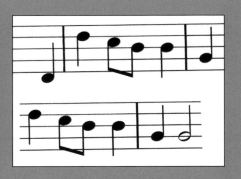

WHAT IS BODY LANGUAGE?

Body language is a series of gestures and movements that people make with their faces, heads, arms, hands, and whole body, to signal thoughts and feelings. Head and facial gestures can say a lot about how a person feels. How often do you raise your eyebrows when you are surprised? Or nod your head when you say "yes"? Body language shows how we feel. People who are tired tend to hunch over and appear smaller than they are. People who are excited and happy make big, confident gestures.

Whole body gestures, meaning the way we stand or sit, can also communicate a lot. For example, confident people show they are sure of themselves by standing up straight. By contrast, people who are insecure or shy avoid eye contact with others.

FACT FILE

People's gestures often mean different things in different countries. In some countries, people shake hands when they greet each other. In other countries, people rub noses to say *hello* or *goodbye*.

HOW SENSITIVE IS HEARING?

Sound is measured in decibels (dB). We can hear sounds ranging from a low rumble to a high-pitched whistle. The lowest sounds can sometimes be felt in the chest, while very shrill sounds may be so high that we cannot actually hear them. A bat's squeak is at the limit of what human beings can hear, and many people cannot hear this noise at all.

Our hearing is not very sensitive compared to that of animals, such as dogs. Dogs can hear very high-pitched sounds. They are able to respond to a supersonic whistle that cannot be heard by human beings at all.

FACT FILE

When you fly in an airplane, your ears may pop as the air inside them expands. If this did not happen, your eardrum would burst as the air trapped inside your ear expanded.

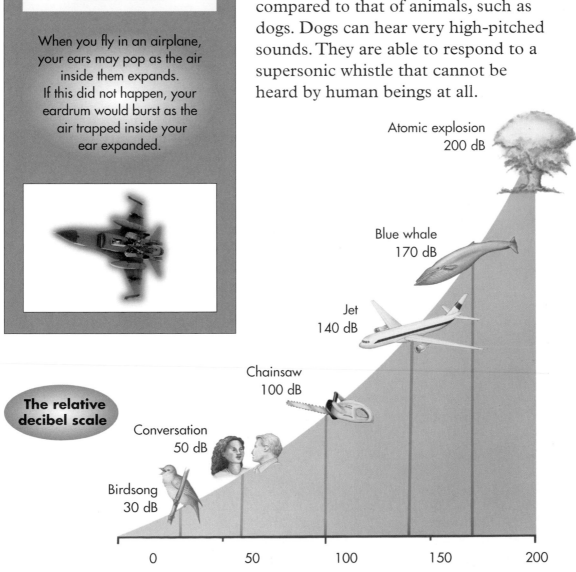

The relative decibel scale

Atomic explosion
200 dB

Blue whale
170 dB

Jet
140 dB

Chainsaw
100 dB

Conversation
50 dB

Birdsong
30 dB

0   50   100   150   200

HOW SIMILAR ARE TASTE AND SMELL?

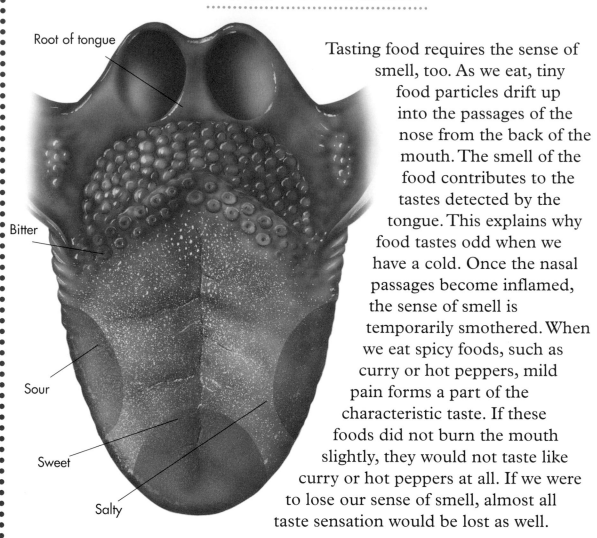

Root of tongue

Bitter

Sour

Sweet

Salty

Tasting food requires the sense of smell, too. As we eat, tiny food particles drift up into the passages of the nose from the back of the mouth. The smell of the food contributes to the tastes detected by the tongue. This explains why food tastes odd when we have a cold. Once the nasal passages become inflamed, the sense of smell is temporarily smothered. When we eat spicy foods, such as curry or hot peppers, mild pain forms a part of the characteristic taste. If these foods did not burn the mouth slightly, they would not taste like curry or hot peppers at all. If we were to lose our sense of smell, almost all taste sensation would be lost as well.

FACT FILE

When we sneeze, a cloud of tiny water droplets is ejected violently into the air through the mouth and nose. This is how colds and influenza are spread.

How do we smell?

As we breathe in, air passes through a cavity behind the nose which contains millions of smell receptors called *olfactory cells*. Sensory hairs, called *cilia*, stick out from the surface of these receptor cells. These hairs detect smells and pass information along nerve fibers to the brain. Substances that we recognize as having an odor dissolve in the layer of mucus covering the sensory cells, stimulating them to produce a signal. Most people are able to detect around 4,000 different smells.

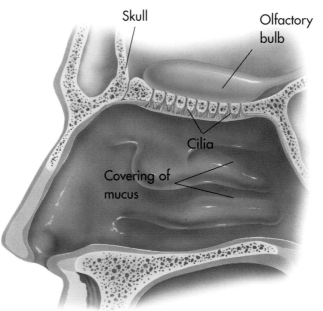

Skull

Olfactory bulb

Cilia

Covering of mucus

FACT FILE

The sense of smell is highly developed in dogs. Some dogs are able to identify and follow the smell of a person's perspiration, even if it is several days old. These dogs are used to find people buried under avalanches or in houses destroyed by earthquakes. They are also trained to sniff out drugs.

However, people whose work is based on their ability to smell, such as chefs, perfume makers, and wine tasters, can distinguish as many as 10,000 different smells.

HOW DO WE RECOGNIZE A SPECIFIC TASTE?

Tastes are detected by thousands of taste buds scattered along the tip, sides, and back of the tongue. There are also some taste buds near the lips, on the roof and sides of the mouth, and in the upper throat. Each taste bud is tiny and contains a microscopic bunch of about 50 cells, which have furry, frilly tips. There are four main types of taste: sweet, sour, salty, and bitter. These can be detected by different areas of the tongue as shown in the diagram opposite. When molecules land on the frilly tip, the taste bud cells make nerve signals. These signals pass along small nerves, which gather into two main nerves–the seventh and ninth cranial nerves. These signals then travel along them to the gustatory, or taste, area in the brain.

The tongue

Cross-section of a Salivary gland showing drops of saliva

FACT FILE

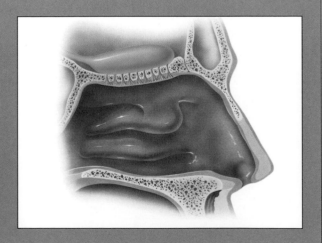

Smells enter the cavity behind the nose when you inhale. They also rise up from the back of the mouth as you eat, which is why smell is such an important part of enjoying food.

WHEN DO WE LOSE OUR SENSE OF TASTE?

Epiglottis

Base of the tongue

Cross-section of a vallate papilla

Taste bud

Salivary glands

FACT FILE

Human beings' sense of taste is less sensitive than that of dogs but their sense of taste may also decline with age. This occurs because the number of taste bud cells manufactured is less, so they send fewer messages to the brain.

Compared to other senses, especially smell, our taste sense is not very sensitive. It has been estimated that a person needs 25,000 times more of a substance in the mouth in order to taste it than to smell it. If we were to lose our sense of smell, almost all taste sensation would be lost as well. We sometimes lose our sense of taste when we have a cold, because our nasal passages become blocked. Gradually, we will lose our sense of taste as we grow older. This may be one reason why elderly people may lose interest in enjoying certain foods.

HOW IS THE EYE MADE?

The eye is like a camera with a "shutter" that lets in light, a lens that focuses the image, and light-sensitive chemicals (just like film) on which the image is registered.

The eye itself is ball-shaped with a slight bulge at the front. In the middle of the eye is a hole called the *pupil*, which opens into the inner dark region of the eye. Light passes through the pupil to the lens, which focuses the light to create a picture at the back of the eyeball.

About 130,000,000 light-sensitive cells communicate this picture to the brain. Light falling on one of these cells causes a chemical change, starting an impulse in the eye fiber called the *retina*. This sends a message down the optic nerve to the seeing part of the brain. The brain is able to interpret this message, and that way we know what we are seeing.

FACT FILE

People with normal vision are able to see shapes in this diagram. People who are color-blind will only be able to see colored dots.

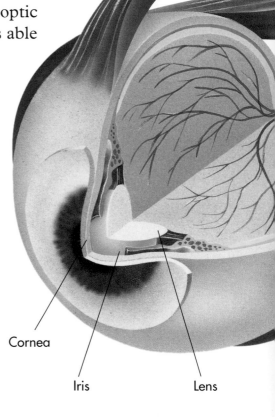

Cornea

Iris

Lens

A cross-section of the human eye

HOW DO WE SEE IN COLOR?

The retina is filled with a layer of tiny cells calls *rods* and *cones*. These cells contain colored substances that react when light falls on them, triggering a nerve impulse.

Rods are slim cells that enable us to see in black and white. They work even if the light is very poor, seeing everything in shades of gray.

Cone cells give us color vision. They contain different light-sensitive substances that respond to either red, yellow-green, or blue-violet light. Together with the gray images produced from the rods, cone cells give you the colored picture that you see.

Cones can only work in bright light, which is why colors are so hard to see in dim light.

Each eye has 125 million rod cells and 7 million cone cells.

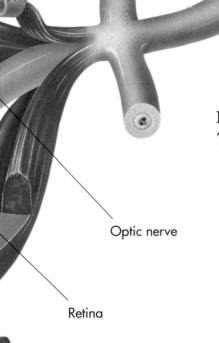

Optic nerve

Retina

FACT FILE

The rod and cone receptor cells are buried in the retina. They are attached to nerves in order to pass on information as they detect light when it falls on them. The mass of rod and cone cells in our eyes is like an organized network of electrical wiring.

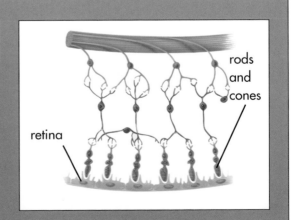

rods and cones

retina

WHAT IS THE RETINA?

When light rays have passed through the eye's cornea and lens, they shine onto the rear inner surface of the eyeball, a layer called the *retina*. It is not much bigger than a postage stamp and is even thinner. Yet, it contains more than 130 million microscopic cells. When light shines on them, they generate nerve signals because they are light sensitive. There are two types of light-sensitive cells in the retina, rods and cones. They are named after their shapes. There are about 125 million rods, and they respond to all types of light, regardless of whether it is white, red, blue, green, or yellow. Rods work in very weak light, so they help the eye to see in dim conditions. The other type of light-sensitive cell is the cone. There are about 7 million cones in the retina, clustered mainly around the back of the eye, opposite the lens.

The retina

Retinal coat

Rod cells

Cone cells

Bipolar cells

Ganglia

Fovia

FACT FILE

The images that we see linger for a fraction of a second on the retina and in the brain. This means that if images change very quickly, each merges or blurs into the next, so we see them as one smooth, continuous moving scene.

WHAT MAKES THE EYEBALL MOVE?

Eye muscles (left eye)

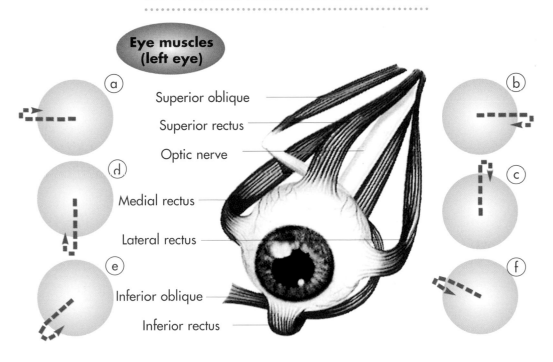

(a)
(b)
(d)
(c)
(e)
(f)

Superior oblique
Superior rectus
Optic nerve
Medial rectus
Lateral rectus
Inferior oblique
Inferior rectus

FACT FILE

The eyes are the body's windows to the world and need special protection. Every second the eyelids blink and sweep tear fluid across the eye, washing away dust and germs. Eyebrows stop water from dripping into the eyes. Eyelashes keep out the dust.

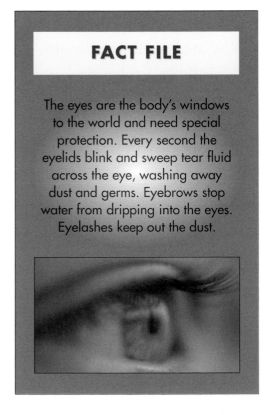

There are six muscles that control the movements of each eye. Muscle (a) swivels it away from the nose; (b) swivels it toward the nose; (c) rotates it upwards; (d) rotates it downwards; (e) moves it down and outwards; (f) moves it upwards and outwards. All these movements are coordinated in the brain. If the lateral rectus muscle in one eye contracts, the medial rectus of the other will contract to a similar extent. The superior recti work together to pull the eyes back and also to look up. The inferior recti make the eyes look down. The superior oblique muscles rotate the eye downwards and outwards, and the inferior oblique muscles rotate the eye upwards and outwards.

WHAT IS PUPIL REFLEX?

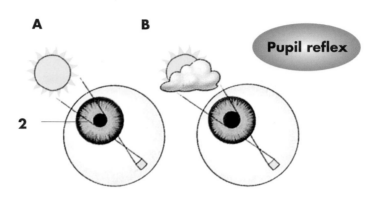

A   B

Pupil reflex

2

The eye muscles contract to make the pupil smaller in bright-light conditions. This stops too much light from getting into the eye and damaging its delicate inner parts. The retina is very sensitive to light. Too much light (as in diagram A) distorts what we see. The pupils vary in size and thus reduce or increase the amount of light entering the eye. Bright light causes a reflex nervous reaction, controlled by areas in the midbrain. The circular pupillary muscle (*1*) in both irises contracts and the radial strands (*2*) extend, thus narrowing the diameter.

Poor light (as in diagram B) will make both pupils dilate, allowing sufficient light to stimulate the cells in the retina (*3*).

FACT FILE

Did you know that the human eye is so sensitive that a person sitting on top of a hill on a moonless night could see a match being struck up to 50 miles away.

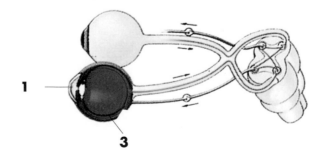

1

3

WHAT IS THE FOCUSING MECHANISM IN THE EYE?

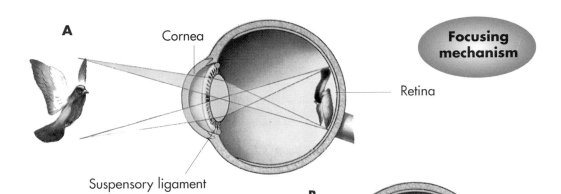

A

Cornea

Retina

Focusing mechanism

Suspensory ligament

B

Lens

Ciliary muscle

The lens of the eye is shaped like the lens in a camera and does a similar job. It adds to the focusing power of the cornea and makes adjustments, depending on whether the object is near or far away. The eye's lens is slightly elastic. It focuses by changing shape. The light rays travel through the lens and the clear jelly in the middle of the eyeball to the retina. In distant vision (as in diagram A), the muscles relax and the ligaments pull the lens into a disc shape. Close vision (as in diagram B) requires a more circular lens, so the muscles constrict and the ligaments relax.

FACT FILE

Why do we have two eyes? Close one eye. Hold a pencil in one hand. Stretch out your arm in front of you and try to touch something. Can you do it? Two eyes working together help you see how close things really are.

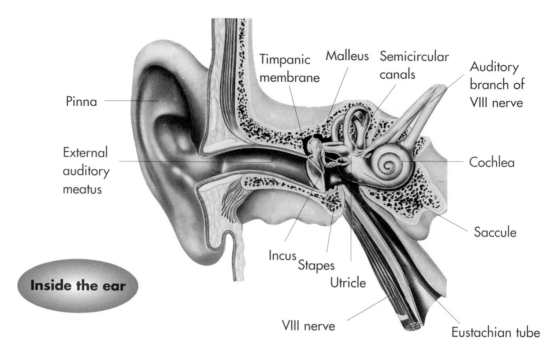

Pinna

Timpanic membrane

Malleus

Semicircular canals

Auditory branch of VIII nerve

External auditory meatus

Cochlea

Saccule

Incus

Stapes

Utricle

VIII nerve

Eustachian tube

Inside the ear

WHAT ARE THE PARTS OF THE EAR?

Hearing involves much more than the outer ears that you see on the side of your head. The ear is actually made up of three parts. The *outer ear* collects sound waves, which are vibrations in the air. The *middle ear* transports these vibrations to the ear drum in the inner ear. There they change into vibrations in fluid, and then into electrical nerve signals. The *inner ear* also gives us our sense of balance. The middle and inner ears are protected from damage by skull bones. The hairs and waxy lining of the outer ear canal protect the ear by gathering and removing dust and germs.

FACT FILE

When you go up in an elevator or fly in an airplane, your ears may pop as the air inside them expands. If this did not happen, your eardrums would burst.

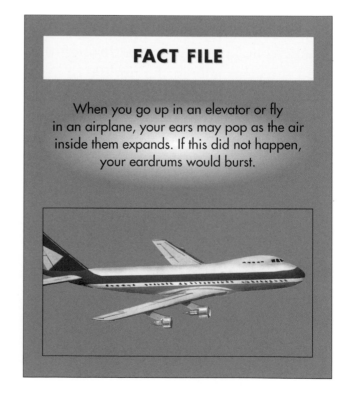

WHAT IS THE COCHLEA?

The hearing portion of the ear is situated at one end of the ear chamber and forms a coil similar to the shell of a snail. It is called the *cochlea*. Throughout its length runs a thin membrane called the *basilar membrane*, which supplies thousands of tiny nerve threads to the cochlea nerve. Changes in the pitch or loudness of sounds are sensed by tiny hairs through which pressure waves travel. When sounds travel into the ear, they make the eardrum inside vibrate or shake. The vibrations pass along a chain of tiny bones called the *hammer*, *anvil*, and *stirrup* and are made louder before passing into the cochlea. The vibrations are then picked up by nerve endings inside the cochlea and changed into messages to send to the brain.

FACT FILE

Loud noises make the eardrum tighten, pulling the stirrup bone away from the cochlea in order to protect the inner ear. Very loud noises can tear the eardrum and cause deafness.

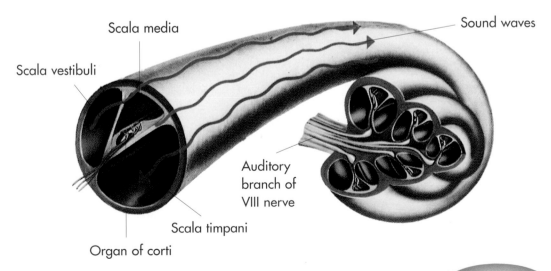

Scala media

Scala vestibuli

Sound waves

Auditory branch of VIII nerve

Scala timpani

Organ of corti

The cochlea

WHEN DO WE SEE IMAGES UPSIDE DOWN?

The eyes are the body's windows to the world. Like a video camera, they detect a moving picture of the world and turn it into tiny electrical signals. These signals are nerve impulses, which go to the brain to be sorted. In ancient times, people thought that light shone out of their eyes onto what they looked at. Now, we know that the opposite occurs. Light rays pass from an object into the eye. Every second or two, the eyelids blink and sweep tear fluid across the conjunctiva, washing away dust and germs.

When light passes through the lens, the image that forms on the retina is actually upside down. This is because of the way in which light rays are bent by the eye's lens. The brain automatically turns the image the right way up, so you are never aware that this is happening.

Anatomy of the eye

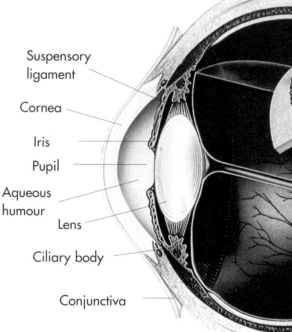

Suspensory ligament

Cornea

Iris

Pupil

Aqueous humour

Lens

Ciliary body

Conjunctiva

FACT FILE

There are six muscles that control the movements of each eye. Muscle (a) swivels the eye away from the nose; (b) swivels it towards the nose; (c) rotates it upward; (d) rotates it downward; (e) moves it down and outwards; (f) moves it upward and outward.

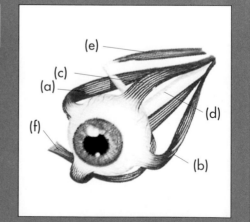

WHAT ARE CONTACT LENSES?

If the eye is not exactly the right shape or if the lens cannot focus properly, you cannot form a clear image on the retina. In this case, you may need to wear eyeglasses to correct your vision. A near-sighted person can see nearby objects very clearly. A far-sighted person can clearly see things in the distance but nearby objects are blurred.

Contact lenses are an alternative to wearing glasses and many people prefer them. Contact lenses are thin plastic discs that rest on the surface of the cornea. They act like the lenses of ordinary glasses. Most modern contact lenses are made from very soft material that does not cause discomfort to the eye. Some lenses are worn only for one day, and then they are thrown away. It can be difficult to get used to wearing contact lenses and to putting them in the eye without scratching the delicate cornea. However, many people now prefer them to wearing glasses.

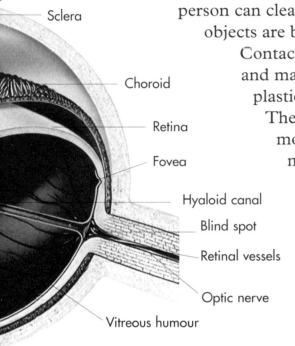

Sclera

Choroid

Retina

Fovea

Hyaloid canal

Blind spot

Retinal vessels

Optic nerve

Vitreous humour

Ocular muscle

FACT FILE

Film and television images consist of a series of rapidly changing still images, yet we see them as continuous motion. There is a slight delay between each of the images that appear on the screen. However, because this delay is so short, our brain is able to fill in the gaps and provide a complete picture of what is happening.

WHAT IS SKIN?

Skin covers the body in a thin layer. In most areas, it is around two-tenths of a centemeter thick. It is thicker on the soles of your feet and on the palms of your hands. Skin is both waterproof and stretchy, and it protects you from the outside world by helping to keep out harmful things like dirt and germs.

Skin has two main layers. The protective outer layer is called the *epidermis*. The skin you see on your body is the top of the epidermis, which is made up of dead cells. New cells are made at the bottom of the epidermis and gradually push their way upwards. The inner layer of the skin is called the *dermis*. The sensory receptors for touch, heat, cold, pressure, and pain are here, as well as the nerve-endings that pick up information and carry it to the brain. The dermis is also where sweat is made and hair grows.

Skin–the protective coat

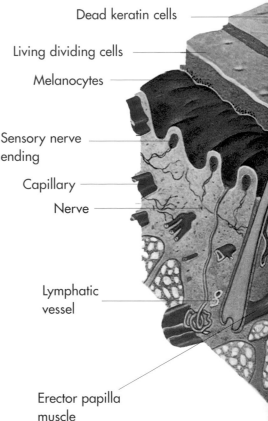

Dead keratin cells

Living dividing cells

Melanocytes

Sensory nerve ending

Capillary

Nerve

Lymphatic vessel

Erector papilla muscle

FACT FILE

Each hair on your body has a tiny erector muscle. When you are cold, these muscles contract to make the hairs stand up, trapping warm air between them and giving you goosebumps.

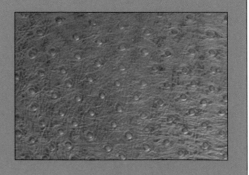

WHAT IS SENSATION?

Your skin is a huge sense organ with thousands of sensory receptors. Skin receptors are sensitive to touch and texture, telling you whether something is smooth or furry, for example. There are also receptors that respond to heat, and ones that respond to cold. Others tell you when something is putting pressure on your skin.

Some skin receptors are sensitive to all four sensations. They are called *free nerve-endings*, and they are thought to send out pain signals if messages from touch, heat, cold, or pressure receptors are too strong. There are free nerve-endings wrapped around the hairs in your skin, sensitive to each hair's slightest movement. Some areas of the skin are densely packed with nerve endings, as in the finger-tips, while others, as those on the back, have comparatively few.

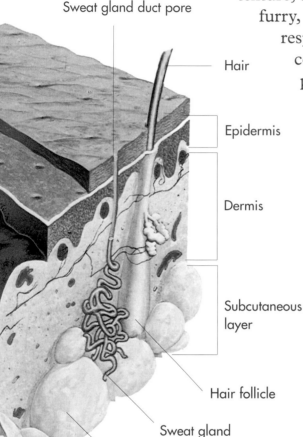

Sweat gland duct pore

Hair

Epidermis

Dermis

Subcutaneous layer

Hair follicle

Sweat gland

Fat cells

FACT FILE

You have other senses besides the five main ones, including those of balance, hunger, and thirst. Your sense of pain is very important. It warns you when your body is hurt or in danger.

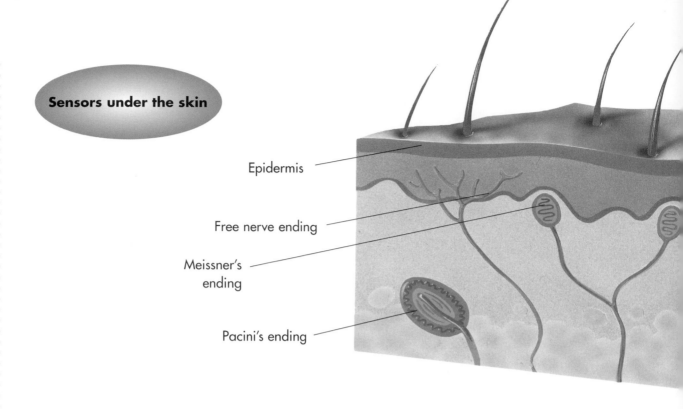

Sensors under the skin

Epidermis

Free nerve ending

Meissner's ending

Pacini's ending

WHY IS TOUCH AN IMPORTANT SENSE?

Your skin is continuously passing huge amounts of information to your brain. It monitors touch, pain, temperature, and other factors that tell the brain exactly how the body is being affected by its environment. Without this constant flow of information, you might injure yourself accidentally. You would be unable to sense whether something was hot, cold, sharp, and so on. This occurs in some rare diseases and in instances of severe burning.

FACT FILE

Did you ever wonder why people are called "touch typists"? This means that they are able to operate typewriter keys without actually looking at them.

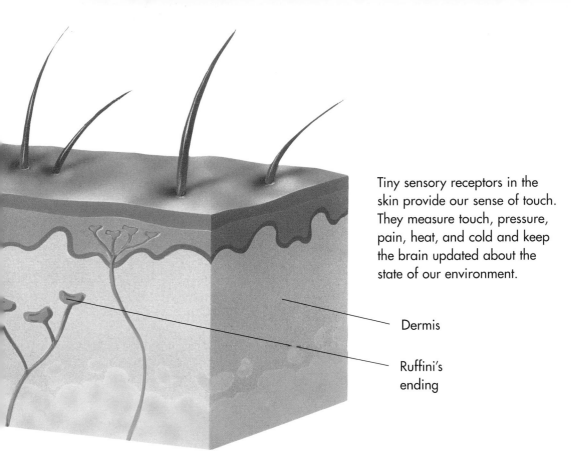

Tiny sensory receptors in the skin provide our sense of touch. They measure touch, pressure, pain, heat, and cold and keep the brain updated about the state of our environment.

Dermis

Ruffini's ending

WHY ARE SOME BODY PARTS MORE SENSITIVE THAN OTHERS?

FACT FILE

The hands are among the body's most sensitive parts. The fingertips are especially sensitive. On one hand there are millions of nerve-endings.

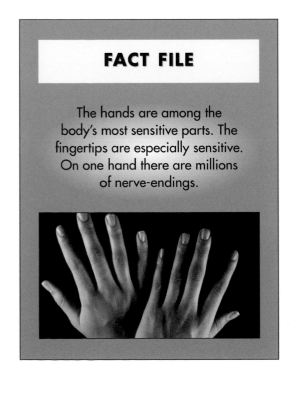

Sensations in the skin are measured by tiny receptors at the ends of nerve fibers. There are several different types of receptors. Each type can detect only one kind of sensation, such as pain, temperature, pressure, touch, and so on. These receptors are grouped together according to the importance of their function. There are large numbers of receptors in the hands and lips, where the sensation of touch is very keen. Your back, however, is far less sensitive since there are fewer receptors in that area of your body.

WHY DO ONIONS MAKE YOU CRY?

When you slice through an onion, you break open a number of onion cells. Some of these cells have enzymes inside of them. When they are sliced open, the enzymes escape. Amino acid is one of the substances that escapes from the onion cells and forms into a volatile gas. This gas reaches your eyes and reacts with the water that keeps the eyes moist. This changes the chemical's form again, producing a mild sulphuric acid that irritates the eyes. The nerve endings in your eyes are very sensitive and so they pick up on this irritation. This is why your eyes sting when you slice onions. The brain reacts by telling your tear ducts to produce more fluid to dilute the irritating acid so the eyes are protected. Your first reaction is probably to rub your eyes, but this will actually make the irritation worse, if there is onion juice on your hands.

FACT FILE

Not all vegetables were always used for food. The ancient Greeks and Romans grew carrots that had thin, tough roots. They used the plants as a medicine but not as a food. Carrots contain carotene, a substance used by the human body to produce vitamin A. Because vitamin A helps prevent visual defects, people say eating carrots is good for the eyes.

WHAT IS AN OPTICAL ILLUSION?

Optical illusions are tricks that our eyes can play on us. Sometimes, they involve seeing the same image in two different ways or seeing images as bigger or smaller than they really are. Unlike a camera or a pair of binoculars, our vision is not a mechanical process. The eye may take in the information, but the brain may interpret it differently. Below are two optical illusions.

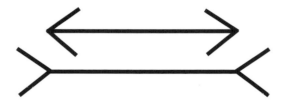

WHICH LINE IS LONGER?

(Both lines are the same length.)

IS THE MIDDLE CIRCLE ON THE LEFT BIGGER?

(No, both middle circles are the same size.)

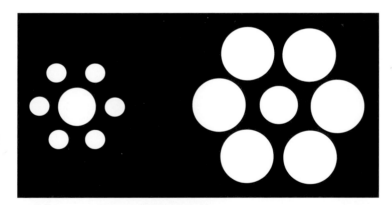

FACT FILE

Our minds can play tricks on us. We see things in the light of experience. Unless our mind can use the clues it has learned to interpret, we can become very confused. For example, how many legs does this elephant have?

Bones and

Muscles

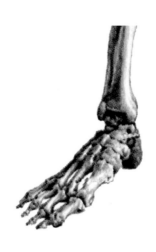

CONTENTS

WHAT ARE SYNOVIAL JOINTS? 34
WHAT DOES A TENDON SHEATH PROTECT? 35

WHICH BONES FORM THE PELVIS? 36
HOW MANY MUSCLES ARE THERE IN THE HUMAN BODY? 37

WHERE ARE THE SMOOTH MUSCLES FOUND? 38
WHAT IS BONE MADE OF? 39

HOW DO MUSCLES WORK? 40
HOW DO JOINTS WORK? 41

HOW DO MUSCLES WORK IN PAIRS? 42
HOW DO MUSCLES RESPOND TO ACTIVITY? 43

HOW DOES A BROKEN BONE HEAL? 44
HOW DO CUTS HEAL? 45

WHEN IS CONNECTIVE TISSUE NEEDED? 46
WHEN ARE DIFFERENT JOINTS USED? 47

WHAT IS YOUR ACHILLES TENDON? 48
WHERE IS YOUR OCCIPITAL BONE? 49

WHERE IS THE SMALLEST BONE IN YOUR BODY? 50
WHERE IS THE MANDIBLE? 51

WHERE IS THE COCCYX LOCATED? 52
WHAT ARE THE METACARPALS? 53

WHERE ARE THE VERTEBRAE? 54
WHERE IS THE HUMERUS BONE? 55

WHERE IS THE LARGEST JOINT IN THE BODY? 56
WHERE IS THE LARGEST MUSCLE IN THE BODY? 57

WHY DO WE HAVE A SKELETON? 58
WHY ARE X-RAYS TAKEN? 59

WHY IS EXERCISE GOOD FOR US? 60
WHY IS SWIMMING SUCH GOOD EXERCISE? 61

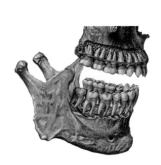

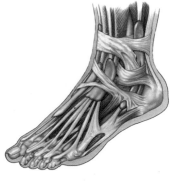

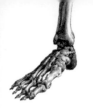

WHAT ARE SYNOVIAL JOINTS?

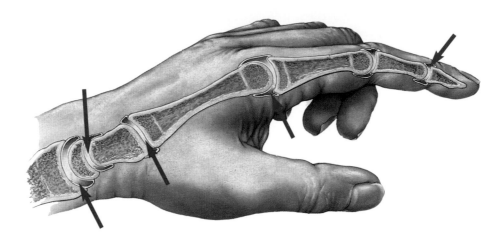

Synovial joints, such as the elbow, knuckles, and wrists, are designed to allow a wide range of motion. They are lined with a slippery coating called *synovium*. Some joints in the body allow only a small amount of movement between the bones. If this occurs with many joints in close proximity, the result is greater flexibility. The bones in the wrist, ankle, and spinal column all work like this. In the synovial joint, the ends of the bones are held together by tough straps called *ligaments*. Cartliage between the bone ends allows them to slide past each other with very little friction.

FACT FILE

The knee is unusual because it has straps of ligaments called *cruciate* (cross-shaped) ligaments inside the joint, as well as ligaments outside. It also has two crescent-shaped pieces of cartilage called *menisci*, that "float" between the bone ends.

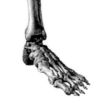

WHAT DOES A TENDON SHEATH PROTECT?

The tendon sheath is a double-walled sleeve designed to isolate, protect, and lubricate the tendon to reduce the possibility of damage from pressure or friction. The space between the two layers of the tendon sheath contains fluid so that these layers slide over each other easily. A strong white cord that links the muscles and bones is called the *tendon* (or *sinew*). It allows muscles to move the bones by pulling on it.

A tendon is a cordlike bundle of connective tissue. Sometimes round in structure and sometimes flat or long, the tendon is woven into the bone at one end and attached to the muscle at the other. Like a limb moving in clothing, the tendon is able to slide up and down within a sheath of fibrous tissue. Tendons at the ankle and wrist are enclosed in sheaths at the points where they cross or are in close contact with other structures.

Tendon sheath

Tendons

FACT FILE

Most muscles can be controlled by consciously thinking about them. They move when you want them to. They are called *voluntary muscles*, and there are more than 600 of them in your body. We use 200 voluntary muscles every time we take a step.

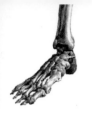

WHICH BONES FORM THE PELVIS?

The pelvis is formed by two large symmetrical hip bones, which are joined in front as the pubic symphysis. In the back, they are attached firmly to the sacrum. In adults, each hip bone appears to be one solid bone, but in fact, they consist of three bones, the ilium, ischium, and pubis, that bind together as the body grows. When you put your hand on your hip, the broad, flat bone you feel is the ilium. Sitting down, your weight rests on the ischium.

Supporting the lower abdomen, the pelvis is a bony structure surrounding the urinary bladder, the last portion of the large intestine, and in females, the reproductive organs. Hence, a woman's pelvis is broader and flatter than a man's with a larger central cavity.

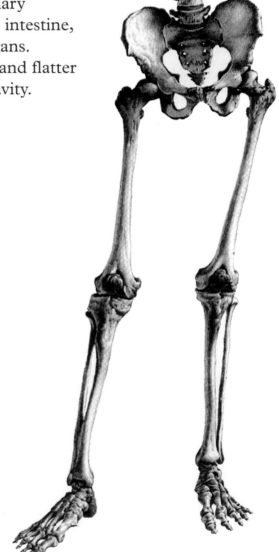

FACT FILE

The pelvis is joined to the spinal column at the sacroiliac joints. The lower part of the pelvis connects wth the thigh bones, or femurs, via ball-and-socket hip joints, enabling the legs to move in various positions.

Ball and socket joint

HOW MANY MUSCLES ARE THERE IN THE HUMAN BODY?

There are over 600 major muscles in the human body. These muscles are divided into two main types, skeletal muscles and smooth muscles. A third type, which shares characteristics with skeletal and smooth muscles and is found only in the heart, is called a *cardiac muscle*.

Skeletal muscles hold the bones of the skeleton together, enable the body to move, and give it its shape. They form a large part of the face, neck, abdomen, arms, and legs. The larger the job it performs, the larger the muscle. So, muscles can vary in size from the large thigh muscles to the small and very weak eye muscles.

FACT FILE

Cardiac muscle makes up the walls of the heart. When cardiac muscle cells contract, they push blood out of the heart and into the arteries.

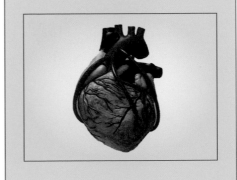

WHERE ARE THE SMOOTH MUSCLES FOUND?

The smooth muscles work slowly and automatically in a natural, rhythmic way. By contracting and then relaxing, they control our many body processes. For example, the steady action of these muscles in the stomach and intestines moves food along for digestion. Smooth muscles are found in the walls of the stomach, intestines, blood vessels, and bladder. Because they are not consciously controlled by the brain, they are involuntary muscles. They react to stimuli from particular nerves that are part of the autonomic nervous system and also to the effects of certain body chemicals.

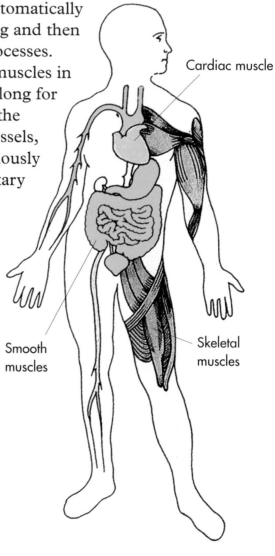

Cardiac muscle

Smooth muscles

Skeletal muscles

FACT FILE

Muscle cells are excitable because the membrane of each cell is electrically charged. Thus, a muscle cell is said to have electric potential.

WHAT IS BONE MADE OF?

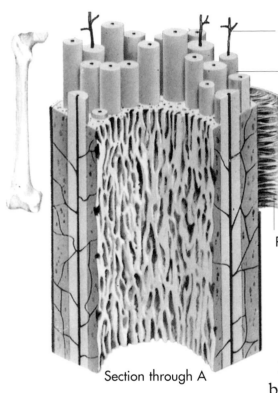

Blood and lymph vessels in central canal

Haversian system

Bone formation

Periosteum

Section through A

A typical bone is made of two types of bony tissue. On the outside is a type of "skin" called the *periosteum*. Below this is a thin layer of thick, dense, "solid" bone. It is known as hard or compact bony tissue. Inside this, and forming the bulk of the middle of the bone, is a different bony tissue, more like a sponge or honeycomb. It has gaps and spaces, and it is called *spongy*, or *alveolar*, *bony tissue*. It is much lighter than the outer compact bone, and the spaces are filled with blood vessels and jelly-like bone marrow for making new blood cells.

FACT FILE

There are 206 bones in the average body. However, there are a few people who have more, such as an extra pair of ribs, making 13 pairs instead of 12, and therefore 208 bones in total.

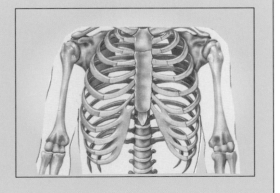

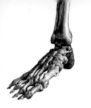

HOW DO MUSCLES WORK?

There are 639 muscles in the human body, each one comprising about ten million muscle cells. Each of these cells is like a motor containing ten cylinders in a row. The cylinders are tiny boxes that contain fluid. When a muscle contracts, the brain sends a message to these tiny boxes. For a fraction of a second, the fluid in the tiny box congeals; then, it becomes fluid again. It is this action that causes the muscle to move. When a muscle is stimulated into action, it reacts quickly. It may contract in less than one tenth of a second. But before it has time to relax, another message comes along. It contracts again and again. All these contractions take place so quickly that they become fused into one action. The result is that the muscle performs one smooth, continuous action.

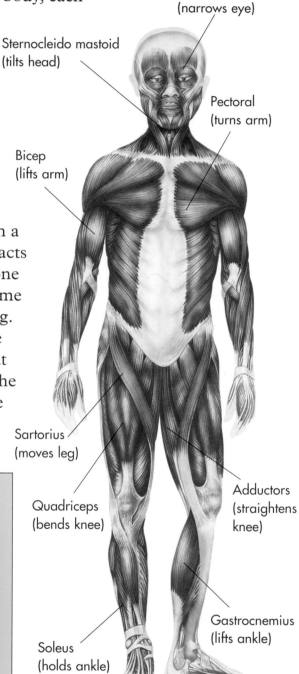

Orbicularis oculi
(narrows eye)

Sternocleido mastoid
(tilts head)

Pectoral
(turns arm)

Bicep
(lifts arm)

Sartorius
(moves leg)

Adductors
(straightens knee)

Quadriceps
(bends knee)

Gastrocnemius
(lifts ankle)

Soleus
(holds ankle)

FACT FILE

When two muscles work against each other, they are always slightly contracted. This is called *muscle tone*. Active people tend to have better muscle tone.

HOW DO JOINTS WORK?

The human body has more than 100 joints. Some joints move like a simple hinge, such as those in the elbows and knees. Other joints move in all directions, such as the shoulder joint or the base of the thumb. Joints in the spine allow only a small amount of movement. The ends of most bones are covered with tough rubbery cartilage, which cushions them from impact as we move. Many joints are lubricated with an oily liquid called *synovial fluid* so they can bend freely. Synovial fluid is held in a bladder between the layers of cartilage on the ends of the bone. These lubricated joints can move freely and without friction.

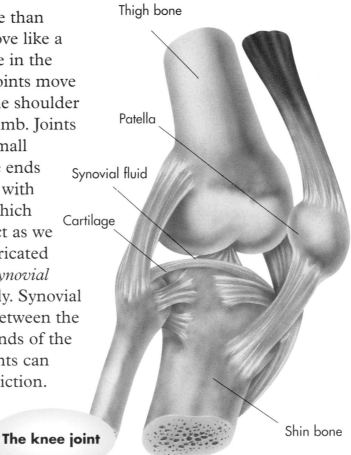

Thigh bone

Patella

Synovial fluid

Cartilage

Shin bone

The knee joint

FACT FILE

Regular exercise improves muscle strength and endurance and keeps the body agile. It can also improve your body shape and posture, as well as strengthening your heart and improving your blood flow. It will generally make you feel better and help you to sleep soundly.

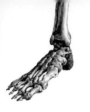

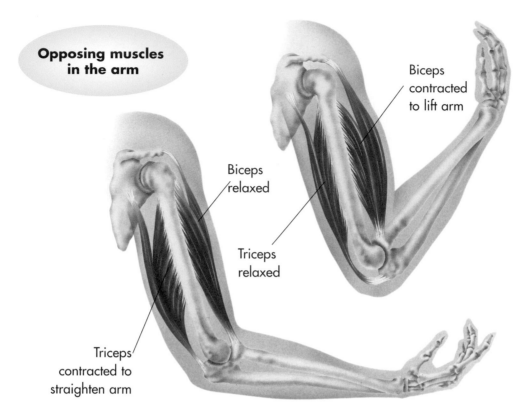

Opposing muscles in the arm

Biceps relaxed

Triceps relaxed

Biceps contracted to lift arm

Triceps contracted to straighten arm

HOW DO MUSCLES WORK IN PAIRS?

Muscles actually work in pairs. A muscle can only pull in one direction. It needs another muscle to pull in the opposite direction in order to return a bone to its original position. When you lift your forearm, the biceps muscle shortens to lift the bone. When you straighten your arm, the triceps muscle pulls it back again, and the biceps muscle relaxes. The same action takes place when you walk or run and when you move your fingers and toes.

FACT FILE

Metabolism is the sum of all chemical activity in our cells, which breaks down the food we take in. Our metabolic rate increases with exercise, which means that we use the energy we get from food much more efficiently.

HOW DO MUSCLES RESPOND TO ACTIVITY?

As a muscle becomes overworked, it produces lactic acid. Lactic acid, along with various toxins that are produced when muscles are active, is carried by the blood through the body and causes tiredness, especially in the brain. The body needs this sensation of fatigue so that it will want to rest. During rest, waste products are removed, the cells recuperate, nerve cells of the brain recharge their batteries, and the joints replace their supplies of the lubricant they have used up. So, while exercise is good for the body and muscles, rest is important too.

FACT FILE

The knee is a typical load-bearing joint. The ends of the bone are cushioned by a pad of cartilage to protect them from impact. Wear and tear is minimized by a lubricant called *synovial fluid*.

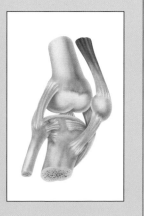

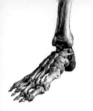

HOW DOES A BROKEN BONE HEAL?

When mending a broken bone, we–or our doctors–are helped in amazing ways by the body itself. The core to this is bone tissue, produced by the connective tissue cells in the broken bone. When a bone is broken, bone and tissue around the break are also damaged, and some of this tissue dies. The entire area around the bone and tissue is held together by a combination of lymph and clotted blood.

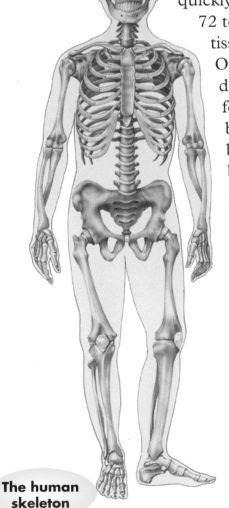

The first stage in repairing a broken bone comes after a few hours when young new tissue cells start to appear. The cells multiply very quickly, becoming filled with calcium. Between 72 to 96 hours after the fracture, they form a tissue, which bonds the ends of the bones. Over the next few months, calcium deposited in the newly formed tissue helps form hard bone. A plaster cast is put on a broken limb to keep the edges of the break in strict alignment, not allowing the bone to move while this process is taking place.

The human skeleton

FACT FILE

Constant use helps to keep the bones strong. Lack of exercise is one of the main reasons why elderly people's bones can become so weak and prone to easy breakage.

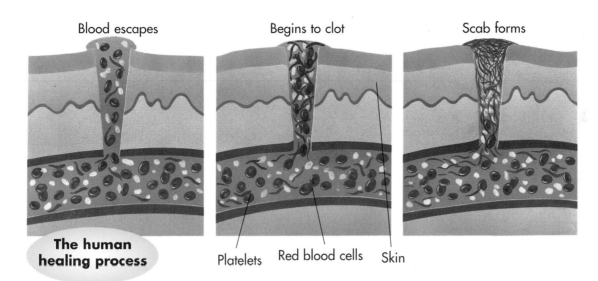

Blood escapes · Begins to clot · Scab forms

The human healing process

Platelets · Red blood cells · Skin

HOW DO CUTS HEAL?

When we cut ourselves, the body is able to heal itself. When the skin incurs a wound, platelets in the blood congregate at the site of the wound to form a temporary clot. This usually happens as soon as a wound is exposed to the air. This quickly plugs the wound.

White blood cells gather around the wound site to kill invading microbes, helping to prevent infection. New cells eventually grow into the wound, replacing the damaged tissue. For a small cut, this usually takes a couple of days. Soon, the clotted material, which has formed a scab, falls off to reveal clean, new skin underneath. Sometimes, we protect our cuts with bandages while our bodies deal with the repair.

FACT FILE

Cells need food, oxygen, and water to survive. Food and water are supplied by blood and other body fluids, which also carry away wastes. Blood also contains food and chemicals needed by the cell.

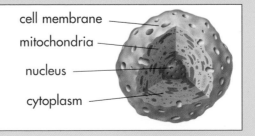

cell membrane
mitochondria
nucleus
cytoplasm

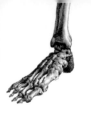

WHEN IS CONNECTIVE TISSUE NEEDED?

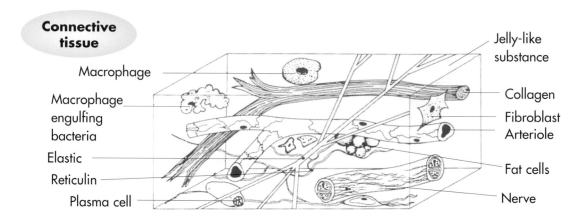

Connective tissue

Macrophage

Macrophage engulfing bacteria

Elastic

Reticulin

Plasma cell

Jelly-like substance

Collagen

Fibroblast
Arteriole

Fat cells

Nerve

The skeleton is the framework of our bodies. It keeps the organs, blood vessels, and nerves in place and also acts as protection. The connective tissue acts as a support to the skeleton and binds it all together. It also supplies the ligaments and tendons for the joints and muscles, holds the larger organs in place, and provides softness for protection and rigidity in the form of cartilage.

There are many forms of connective tissue, but they are all developed from the same jelly-like substance, which is made up of salts, water, protein, and carbohydrates. Inside this jelly are elastic threads to give elasticity, collagen to give strength, reticulin to give support, white cells and macrophages to fight infection, fat cells for storage, and finally plasma cells to produce antibodies.

FACT FILE

The shape and appearance of a cell depends on what job it does. Cells consist of jelly-like cytoplasm, surrounded by a membrane. Nutrients pass through this membrane and substances produced by the cell leave.

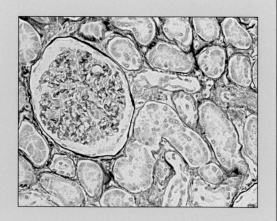

WHEN ARE DIFFERENT JOINTS USED?

A joint is the meeting point between bones. It usually controls the amount of movement. Some joints have to be strong, while others need to be very mobile. As it is not possible for joints to be both strong and mobile, we require many different kinds of joints.

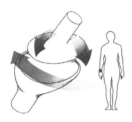

Ellipsoid joint:
Allows circular and bending movement but no rotation.

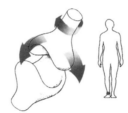

Saddle joint:
Allows movement in two directions but no rotation.

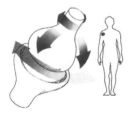

Ball-and-socket joint:
A joint freely moving in all directions.

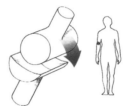

Hinge joint:
Allows extension and flexion.

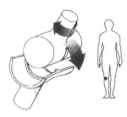

Condylar joint:
This is similar to a hinge joint but with slight rotation to allow the joint to "lock" into an extended position.

Pivot joint:
Allows rotation but no other movement.

FACT FILE

The knee joint is the largest and most complex joint. As it reaches full extension, it rotates slightly and "locks" into a rigid limb from hip to ankle.

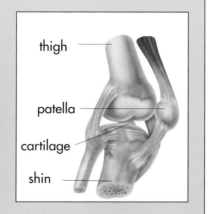

thigh

patella

cartilage

shin

Plane joint:
A flat surface allows the bones to slide on each other, but they are restricted by ligaments to a small range.

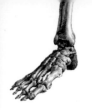

WHAT IS YOUR ACHILLES TENDON?

Tendons are the strong white cords (also called *sinews*) that join muscles to bones. The Achilles tendon, which is one of the strongest tendons in the body, attaches the muscles of the calf to the heel bone. It is located at the back of the ankle. The name is derived from the Greek legend of Achilles, a hero who was killed during the Trojan wars by an arrow in the heel.

Often associated with sports injuries, the Achilles tendon can rupture as the result of a vigorous upward movement of the foot or a blow to the calf when the muscles are contracted. There is a particular vulnerability among people over thirty involved in activities that involve running. A full rupture is usually characterized by a snap and severe pain, after which it is impossible to push off or stand on the toes. If injured, ice should be applied as soon as possible to the back of the ankle, raising the leg so it can't be moved. Often, surgery is required to sew the tendon together, and the injured party will need a month or two off the leg before attempting strengthening or stretching exercises. Full recovery takes a year or more.

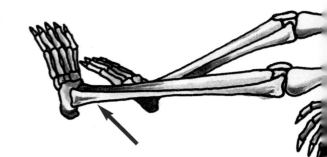

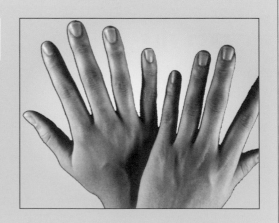

FACT FILE

Thirty-five powerful muscles move the human hand. Fifteen are in the forearm rather than in the hand itself. This arrangement gives great strength to the hand without making the fingers so thick with muscles that they would be difficult to move.

WHERE IS YOUR OCCIPITAL BONE?

A system of muscles and tendons connects the head to the spinal column, the collarbone, and the shoulder blades. These muscles and tendons control the movement of the head. The occipital bone forms the back of the skull. This bone rests on the spinal column and forms a joint on which the head moves. Most of the weight of the head is in front of the occipital bone, and the head is held in an erect position by muscles in the neck. When a person becomes sleepy, these muscles relax, and the head falls forward. Other large bones of the head include the maxilla, the mandible, and the parietal, frontal, sphenoid, and temporal bones.

Muscles in the head are important to the processes of chewing and swallowing. They are also responsible for facial expressions, such as smiling or frowning.

FACT FILE

Repeated activity of the facial muscles, the gradual loss of fat pads under the skin, and the loss of skin elasticity cause wrinkles to form in the faces of older people.

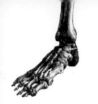

WHERE IS THE SMALLEST BONE IN YOUR BODY?

The smallest bone in the body is called the *stirrup*. It is in the middle ear and is part of the system that carries sound signals to the brain. At only three-tenths of a centemeter long, the stirrup is about the size of a grain of rice. The footplate of the stirrup bone is attached to a membrane called the *oval window*, which leads to the inner ear. It is connected to two other very small bones called the *hammer* and *anvil*. All three of these bones are joined to the eardrum, where sound is collected before it is sent in the form of nerve signals to the brain.

The ear is a very important organ for maintaining balance. Without a sense of balance, we could not hold our body steady, and we would stagger and fall when we tried to move.

FACT FILE

Some people suffer from motion sickness when they travel by boat, car, train, or airplane. Motion sickness is caused by excessive stimulation of the vestibular organs. Researchers do not know why some people develop motion sickness more easily than others do.

WHERE IS THE MANDIBLE?

There are fourteen bones in the face. The two that make up the jaw are the maxillae (upper jaw) and the mandible (lower jaw). The mandible, like the maxilla, contains sockets for the 32 teeth, which are embedded in fibrous tissue. Teeth are hard, bonelike structures in the upper and lower jaws of human beings and many kinds of animals. They are the hardest parts of the body.

Muscles in the head are important to the processes of chewing and swallowing. They are responsible for facial expressions, such as smiling or frowning. A system of muscles and tendons connects the head to the spinal column, the collarbone, and the shoulder blades. These muscles and tendons control the movement of the head.

FACT FILE

The lower jaw is the only bony part of the face that moves. There are 32 permanent teeth, 16 in each jaw. Each jaw has 4 incisors, 2 canines, 4 premolars, and 6 molars.

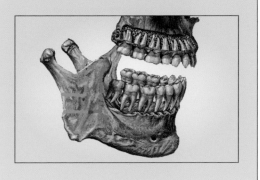

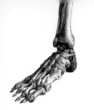

WHERE IS THE COCCYX LOCATED?

The coccyx is located at the base of the spine. The bones of the head, neck, and trunk form the axial skeleton, while the spine forms an axis that supports the other parts of the body. The spine, at the top of which is the skull, is made up of separate bones called *vertebrae* that have fibrous disks between them. The ribs protect the heart and lungs and act as an air box for breathing. There are usually 12 ribs on each side of the body. They are attached to the thoracic vertebrae.

In the lower part of the back lie the five lumbar vertebrae, and below the last of these is located the sacrum, followed by the coccyx.

During childhood, there are four separate bones that make up the coccyx. During later life, the three lowest of these often become fused together, forming a hook-like bone. The point where the sacrum and coccyx actually meet will remain fibrous throughout life.

Coccyx

FACT FILE

The human foot has 26 bones. They are the seven tarsals, or anklebones; the five metatarsals, or instep bones; and the 14 phalanges, or toe bones.

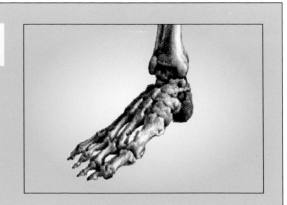

WHAT ARE THE METACARPALS?

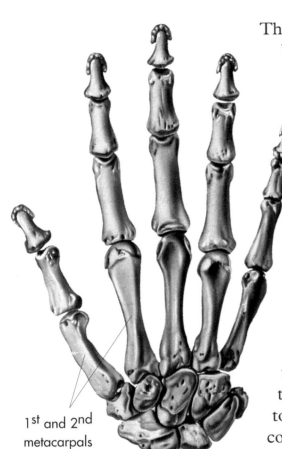

1st and 2nd metacarpals

The metacarpals are one of the 27 bones in the human hand. These are broken down into the wrist bones or *carpals*, the palm bones or *metacarpals*, and the four finger and thumb bones or *phalanges*. The wrist is made up of eight carpal bones that are arranged roughly in two rows. Starting from the thumb side, the row nearest to the forearm contains the scaphoid, lunate, triquetrum, and pisiform bones. The second row has the trapezium, trapezoid, capitate, and hamate bones. The palm is made up of five long metacarpal bones that connect the fingers and thumb to the wrist. Each finger of the hand contains three slender phalanges, while the thumb contains only two.

FACT FILE

Muscles can't push. They can only pull. Muscles are pulling gently against each other most of the time. This keeps them firm and stops them from becoming flabby. Muscles get bigger and stronger if you exercise them. Muscles are joined to bones by tough "bands" called *tendons*.

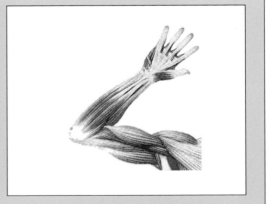

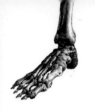

WHERE ARE THE VERTEBRAE?

The spine, which is also known as the *spinal column*, *vertebral column*, or *backbone*, is the part of the skeleton that extends down the middle of the back. It is made up of a column of bones called *vertebrae*. It plays a crucial part in our posture and movement and also protects the all-important spinal cord.

Although some grow together later in life, the human spine basically consists of 33 vertebrae. There are 7 cervical (neck), 12 thoracic (chest), 5 lumbar (lower back), 5 sacral (hip), and 4 coccygeal (tailbone) vertebrae. They are secured in place by a combination of muscles and strong connective tissue called *ligaments*. Most have fibrous intervertebral disks between them in order to absorb shock and enable the spine, which normally has a slight natural curve, to bend.

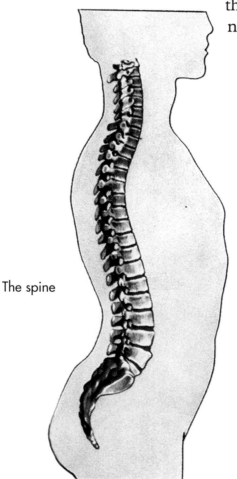

The spine

FACT FILE

Many people suffer from backaches. Sometimes, the intervertebral disk, the tissue that lies between the vertebrae, sticks out and presses on nerves. This condition is called a *slipped disk*. It can cause severe pain in the lower back, thighs, and legs.

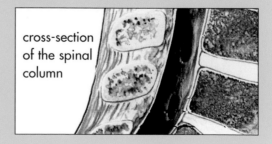

cross-section of the spinal column

WHERE IS THE HUMERUS BONE?

Humerus

The humerus bone is the bone of the upper arm, connected to the bones of the forearm (the radius and ulna) by the elbow joint. The three bone connections in the elbow form three smaller joints, which make possible various movements. The humerus–ulna joint and the humerus–radius joint allow for the bending of the forearm up and down, while the radius–ulna joint and the humerus–radius joint make it possible for a person to rotate the forearm and to turn the palm of the hand up and down. The bones are held in place in the elbow joint by a capsule or pouch of robust connective tissue which surrounds it.

FACT FILE

Excessive or violent twisting of the forearm may injure the elbow ligaments, capsule, or tendons. One such injury, sometimes called *tennis elbow*, often results from playing tennis.

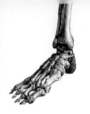

WHERE IS THE LARGEST JOINT IN THE BODY?

The knee joint is the largest and most complex joint in the body. The knee is the joint where the thighbone meets the large bone of the lower leg. The knee moves like a hinge, but it can also rotate and move a little from side to side. The knee is more likely to be damaged than most other joints because it is subject to tremendous forces during vigorous activity. Most of the knee injuries that occur in football and other sports result from twisting the joint. The knee ligaments are the strongest connections between the femur and the tibia. Ligaments keep the bones from moving out of position.

Patella

Tibia

Fibula

FACT FILE

The patella (or kneecap) is a small, flat, triangular bone in front of the joint. It is not directly connected with any other bone. Muscle attachments hold it in place.

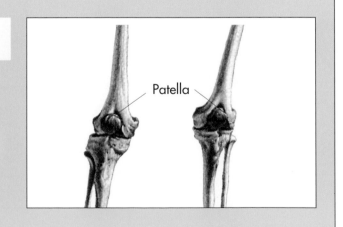

Patella

WHERE IS THE LARGEST MUSCLE IN THE BODY?

The largest muscle in the human body is called the *gluteus maximus*, and this is situated in the buttocks. The smallest muscle is the stapedius, which can be found in the middle ear. A muscle is the tough, elastic tissue that enables body parts to move. Muscles are found throughout the body. As a person grows, the muscles get bigger. Muscle makes up nearly half the body weight of an adult.

Of over 600 muscles in the human body, no less than 240 have specific names. They fall into two main categories, skeletal muscles and smooth muscles. A third type, called *cardiac muscle*, can be found only in the heart. It has similrities to both the skeletal and smooth muscles. People use muscles to make various movements.

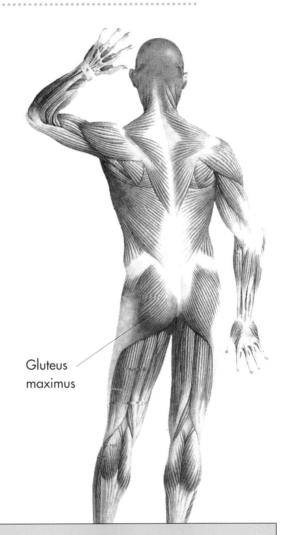

Gluteus maximus

FACT FILE

The longest muscle is the sartorius, which runs from the side of the waist, diagonally down across the front of the thigh to the inside of the knee. Among the most powerful muscles are the masseters, one on each side of the face.

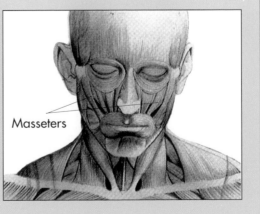

Masseters

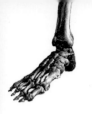

WHY DO WE HAVE A SKELETON?

A skeleton is made up of a network of bones. Bones provide a framework that holds the whole body together.

Without a skeleton, we would have no support and would simply flop about like a rag doll. This would mean that we would not be able to move about.

The skeleton also gives protection to the delicate organs in our bodies, such as the brain, heart, and lungs. It acts as a support to all the soft parts of the body. The skeleton also provides a system of levers that the muscles can work on, enabling us to carry out all our movements.

FACT FILE

At birth, a baby has 300 bones, but 94 join together in early childhood. Your hand and wrist alone contain 27 bones.

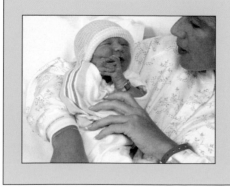

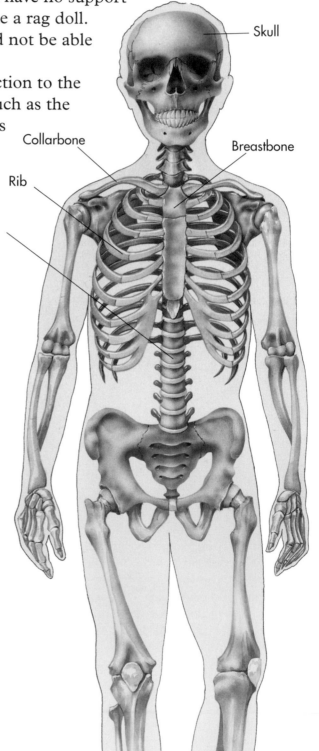

Skull

Collarbone

Breastbone

Rib

Backbone

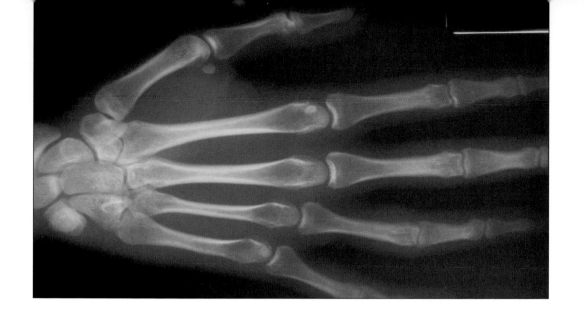

WHY ARE X-RAYS TAKEN?

If we are in an accident, often we go to hospital to have an X-ray taken of our body to see if we have any broken bones. The X-ray is a shadowgraph or shadow picture. X-rays pass through the part of the body being x-rayed and cast shadows on the film. The film is coated with a sensitive emulsion on both sides. After it is exposed, an X-ray is developed like ordinary photographic film. The X-ray does not pass through bones and other objects. It casts denser shadows, which show up as light areas on the film. This will show the doctor whether any bone has been broken or dislocated.

FACT FILE

Like X-rays, ultrasonic sound waves travel into the body and are bounced back by the organs inside. A screen can display the reflected sound as a picture. This is used to scan an unborn baby in the mother's womb.

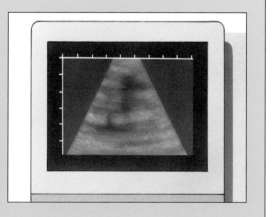

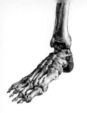

WHY IS EXERCISE GOOD FOR US?

Regular exercise is important because it keeps bones, joints, and muscles healthy. During physical exertion, the rate at which the heart beats increases, and it pumps more oxygenated blood around the body. How quickly the heart rate returns to normal after exercise is one way to assess how fit someone is and how exercise is actually improving their fitness.

Once almost everyone did manual work of some kind. It was essential for survival. Human bodies were not designed for the inactive lives many of us now lead. That is why exercise is important for good health.

FACT FILE

Swimming is a very good form of exercise. It uses lots of muscles without causing strain.

WHY IS SWIMMING SUCH GOOD EXERCISE?

FACT FILE

It is important to stretch your muscles before and after exercise to distribute the lactic acid.

Swimming is an especially good form of exercise because it allows us to stretch nearly all of our muscles while supported in the water. Unlike other forms of exercise, such as running or gymnastics, there are few risks of exercise-related injury. Many who participate in professional sports use swimming as a way of keeping fit while recovering from sports-related injuries. It is important, though, to combine swimming with other forms of exercise, such as cycling and running. All of these are good for the heart and allows you to maintain a good level of all-round fitness.

Heart and

Circulation

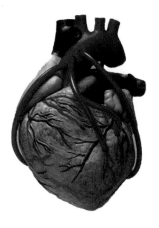

CONTENTS

· ·

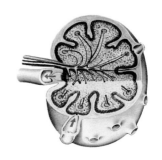

WHERE IS OUR CIRCULATORY SYSTEM? 64
WHAT IS A HEARTBEAT? 65

WHY DOESN'T BLOOD FLOW BACKWARDS? 66
WHERE ARE THE JUGULAR VEINS LOCATED? 67

HOW DOES THE HEART WORK? 68
WHEN IS HEMOPHILIA? 69

WHAT IS CORONARY CIRCULATION? 70
WHAT IS BLOOD MADE FROM? 71

WHY DOES BLOOD CLOT? 72
WHAT IS LYMPH? 73

WHEN DO PEOPLE HAVE HEART ATTACKS? 74
WHEN DOES THE HEART STOP BEATING? 75

WHEN DOES BLOOD FLOW FROM VEINS TO ARTERIES? 76
WHEN DOES THE SPLEEN PRODUCE RED BLOOD CELLS? 77

WHEN ARE BLOOD TYPES DETERMINED? 78
WHEN DO RED AND WHITE BLOOD CELLS DIE? 79

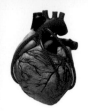

WHERE IS OUR CIRCULATORY SYSTEM?

Heart

Arteries (red)

Veins (blue)

The aortic and pulmonic valves are in the heart. The network that carries blood throughout the body is an amazing natural device known as the *circulatory system*. Not only does it supply the cells of the body with the food and oxygen they need to survive, it carries carbon dioxide and other waste matter away from the cells, helps regulate the body's temperature, and transports elements that protect the body from disease. The network also allows the movement of chemical substances called *hormones*, which help regulate and stabilize the functioning of various parts of the body. The blood vessels, which form a complex system of connecting tubes throughout the body, fall into three major categories. The arteries transport blood from the heart, the veins return the blood back to the heart, and the capillaries are minute vessels that connect the arteries and the veins.

FACT FILE

The three main parts of the human circulatory system are the heart, the blood vessels, and the blood. In addition, a watery fluid called *lymph* and the vessels that carry it are often thought of as part of the circulatory system.

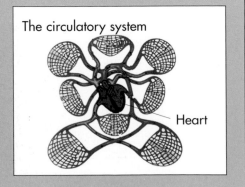

The circulatory system

Heart

WHAT IS A HEARTBEAT?

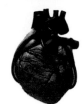

The heart pumps blood on both sides at the same time. The right ventricle contracts, sending blood to the lungs, while the left ventricle contracts and squeezes blood out to the body. There are two stages in the heart's cycle of activity, called *systole* and *diastole*. The systole stage happens when the ventricles contract, and the diastole stage occurs when the ventricles relax and the atria contract. One full cycle of contraction and relaxation makes a heartbeat and is known as the *cardiac cycle*. During every cardiac cycle, the heart valves open and close, and it's the closing of the valves that makes the pulsing sound of a heartbeat. Doctors listen to this with a stethoscope. With the ventricles' contraction, the mitral and tricuspid valves close, creating the first sound. As soon as the valves close, pressure in the ventricles forces the aortic and pulmonic valves to open. After a contraction ends, the ventricle pressure drops and the aortic and pulmonic valves close and cause most of the second heart sound.

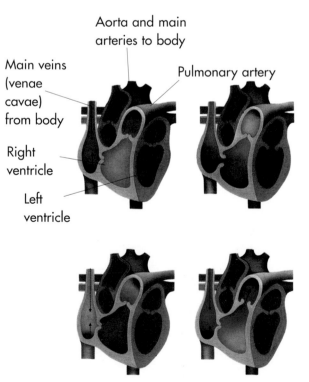

Aorta and main arteries to body

Main veins (venae cavae) from body

Pulmonary artery

Right ventricle

Left ventricle

FACT FILE

The heart of an average person at rest beats 60 to 80 times each minute. Each beat sends about $2^1/_2$ ounces of blood out of each ventricle. This means that at rest the heart pumps some $2^1/_2$ gallons of blood each minute.

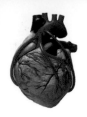

WHY DOESN'T BLOOD FLOW BACKWARDS?

Blood is transported to the heart by means of blood vessels called *veins*. Veins are part of the whole system of blood vessels which circulate blood. The blood in your veins travels quite slowly, and many large veins have valves to stop the blood from draining backwards towards the legs and feet.

Blood flowing forward forces the valve flaps to open (1). Blood flowing backwards forces them to shut (2). The valves in the heart work in exactly the same way.

Blood is also helped along by arm and leg muscle contractions. That is why, if you stand still for a long period of time, blood can collect in your legs and make them puffy and sore.

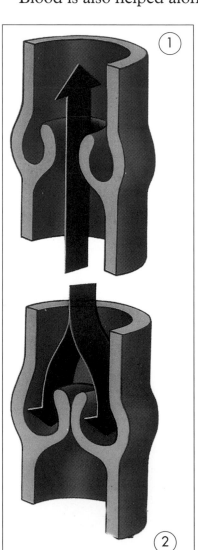

FACT FILE

The lymphatic system is one of the body's defenses against infection. Harmful particles and bacteria that have entered the body are filtered out by small masses of tissue that lie along the lymphatic vessels. These bean-shaped masses are called *lymph nodes*.

WHERE ARE THE JUGULAR VEINS LOCATED?

There are four large veins that return blood to the heart from the head and neck. They are called *jugular veins*. They get their name from the Latin word for collarbone, *jugulus*. The jugular veins are situted on either side of the neck, each side having an external and internal jugular. The external jugulars carry blood from external parts of the head and neck to the heart and are close to the surface. The internal jugulars lie deeper, with blood from the deeper neck tissues of the neck and the interior of the skull. "Going for the jugular" is a well-known phrase, referring to the opening of the much larger internal jugular vein, which usually proves fatal because of the rapid loss of blood that invariably occurs.

FACT FILE

Whiplash is a term commonly used to describe a type of injury to the neck. This kind of injury results from a sudden blow that throws the head rapidly backward and forward.

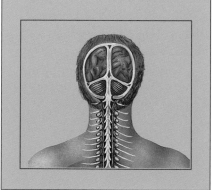

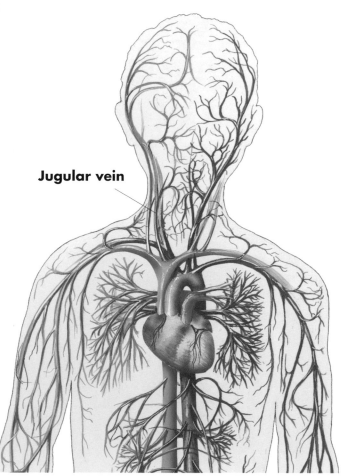

Jugular vein

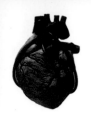

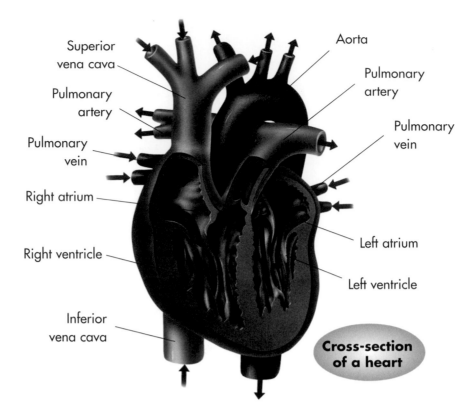

Superior vena cava

Pulmonary artery

Pulmonary vein

Right atrium

Right ventricle

Inferior vena cava

Aorta

Pulmonary artery

Pulmonary vein

Left atrium

Left ventricle

Cross-section of a heart

HOW DOES THE HEART WORK?

The heart is a fist-sized muscular organ that pumps blood around the body. It is actually two pumps that are joined together. At the top of each side of the heart is a thin-walled chamber called the *atrium*, which receives blood that returns to the heart through the veins. Once the atrium is filled with blood, it contracts and squeezes into a much more muscular chamber called the *ventricle*. The ventricle then contracts and forces blood at high pressure along the arteries to the lungs and the rest of the body. A system of one-way valves stops the blood from leaking back into the heart. The left side of the heart pumps blood to the lungs to collect more oxygen.

FACT FILE

An electrocardiogram, or ECG, measures the electrical signals that the heart produces as it beats. These signals change when a person suffers from certain medical conditions that affect the heart. They are measured by attaching wires to the chest near the heart. A doctor can study results as printed information.

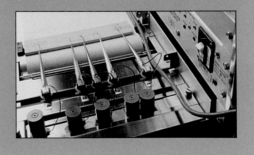

WHAT

....

Blood components

Red blood cells

Blood is the flu
system. Blood
distributes this
regular supply
components a
plasma, in whi
suspended. Th
and large prot
the interstitial
This will eithe
Blood amount
   The red and
plasma occup
water, 7 perce
up of small m

FAC

Blood is warr
the liquid in
system. It abso
the busy parts,
and muscles,
to cooler pa

WHAT IS HEMOPHILIA?

Red blood cells

Hemophilia is an inherited deficiency in which the substance necessary for blood clotting, called *Factor 8*, is missing. This is a painful condition because hemophiliacs can have swollen joints where the blood leaks into them. More seriously, even a slight cut or bump can be dangerous if the bleeding cannot be stopped. The transmission of this condition is sex-linked, as it is carried solely by females but shows symptoms only in males. Sons of a hemophiliac male are normal but daughters, although outwardly normal, may transmit this deficiency to approximately half of their sons.

   This condition can be treated by giving the hemophiliac doses of Factor 8, which has either been extracted from donated blood or has been synthesized in a laboratory.

FACT FILE

When we look at other human bodies, we usually concentrate on the face. Our features are largely inherited, under control of the genes, which is why we resemble our parents.

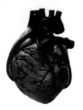
Co
circ

Right cor
artery

C
v

Coror
suppli
huma
semilu
fill wi
blood
heart
coron
tricus
Th
from
amou
a cor
leads

WHY DOES BLOOD CLOT?

When you accidentaly cut yourself, the blood clots to prevent the wound from bleeding. Clotting is caused by substances in the blood. Together with small particles called *platelets*, these substances produce masses of fine mesh when they are exposed to air. They block the wound and prevent more blood loss. New cells grow rapidly into the wound, replacing the damaged tissue. Soon the clotted material, called a *scab*, falls off and clean, new skin is revealed underneath.

FACT FILE

Your blood pressure can be measured by a doctor with a special blood pressure monitor. During sleep, your blood pressure decreases slightly, and during exercise and emotional excitement, it increases.

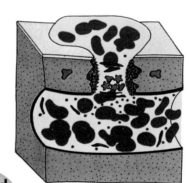
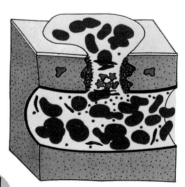
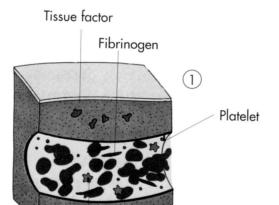
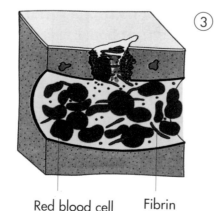

Tissue factor

Fibrinogen

①

Platelet

Stages of blood clotting

Plasma factor

②

③

④

Red blood cell   Fibrin

WHAT IS LYMPH?

Your body's main attack force is called the *lymph system*. Like the blood system, it is a set of vessels, which carry liquid around the body. This liquid is called *lymph*. Lymph contains special white blood cells called *lymphocytes*. These can make substances called *antibodies*, which fight germs and cope with poisons. It works in the following way: The fluid passes out of the capillary (**1**) and either into the vein or into the smallest, thin-walled lymph vessel (**2**). These vessels join together to form large channels and finally reach the thoracic duct running next to the descending aorta. This duct joins one of the main branches of the superior vena cava (**5**). Valves (**3**) keep lymph flowing in one direction. Lymph glands (**4**) are found throughout the body and at places where lymph vessels unite (**6**).

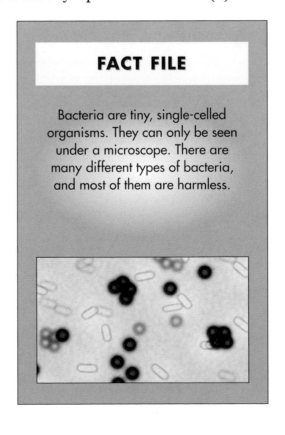

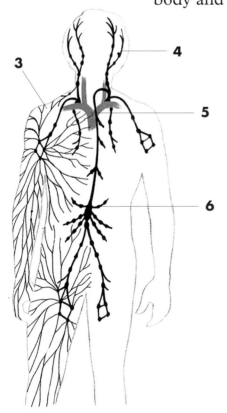

FACT FILE

Bacteria are tiny, single-celled organisms. They can only be seen under a microscope. There are many different types of bacteria, and most of them are harmless.

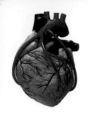

WHEN DO PEOPLE HAVE HEART ATTACKS?

Your heart is a powerful muscle, which pumps blood around your body. It is only the size of your fist and weighs about a pound. Each and every day, it pumps about 4,755 gallons of blood around your body, and yet, you are not normally aware that it is even beating. Run quickly upstairs, though, and you will soon feel it thumping away inside your rib cage.

A heart attack occurs when the inability of either or both sides of the heart are able to pump sufficient blood to meet the needs of our body. Other prominent causes of a heart attack are abnormally high blood pressure (hypertension), coronary atherosclerosis (the presence of fatty deposits in the lining of the coronary arteries), and rheumatic heart disease.

A person with left-sided heart failure experiences shortness of breath after exertion, difficulty in breathing while lying down, spasms of breathlessness at night, and abnormally high pressure in the pulmonary veins. A person with right-sided failure experiences abnormally high pressure in the systemic veins, enlargement of the liver, and accumulation of fluid in the legs. A person with failure of both ventricles has an enlarged heart that beats in gallop rhythm–that is, in groups of three sounds rather than two.

FACT FILE

An electrocardiogram, or ECG, measures the electrical signals that the heart produces as it beats. These signals change when a person is suffering from certain medical conditions that affect the heart.

WHEN DOES THE HEART STOP BEATING?

The heart

Aorta

Superior vena cava

Pulmonary artery

Pulmonary valve

Pulmonary veins

Atria

Aortic valve

Mitral valve

Chordae tendineae

Tricuspid valve

Papillary muscle

Ventricles

Inferior vena cava

Your heart is a muscular pump that never stops beating. It has its own timing device that produces tiny electrical signals. These signals cause the heart muscle to contract rhythmically. The pump on the right side of the heart receives blood that has already been circulated through the body and has used up most of its oxygen. The right pump sends the blood through the lungs. The blood comes back bright red and rich in oxygen to the heart's left side, ready for its journey around the body. When the heart stops beating, body tissues no longer receive fresh blood carrying oxygen and nutrients.

However, in a hospital, a cardiopulmonary machine can temporarily take over the job of the heart and lungs. This allows doctors to carry out operations on the heart, such as replacing diseased valves.

FACT FILE

When the body is very active, the heart can pump 20 gallons of blood each minute. That would fill a bathtub within two minutes.

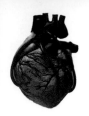
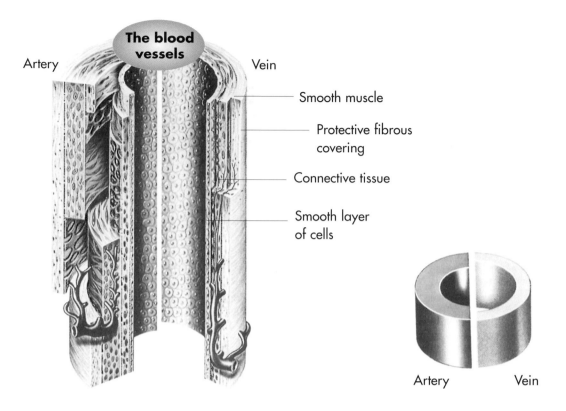

The blood vessels

Artery

Vein

Smooth muscle

Protective fibrous covering

Connective tissue

Smooth layer of cells

Artery   Vein

WHEN DOES BLOOD FLOW FROM VEINS TO ARTERIES?

Your body has an amazingly complex and delicate system of blood vessels, carrying blood to all parts of the body and then returning it to the heart. These vessels are called *arteries* and *veins*, and they are both tubes made up of four different layers. The arteries carry the blood away from the heart, and the veins return it.

The veins frequently anastomose (or join together) with each other so that the blood flow can alter direction. This is caused if there is any constriction or pressure from movement of muscles or ligaments.

FACT FILE

Just over half of blood is plasma, which contains hundreds of dissolved substances, from sugars for energy to hormones to wastes like carbon dioxide.

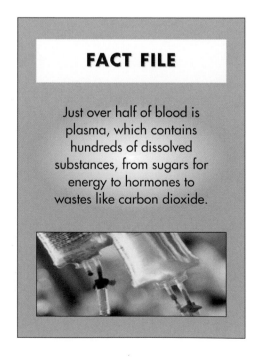

WHEN DOES THE SPLEEN PRODUCE RED BLOOD CELLS?

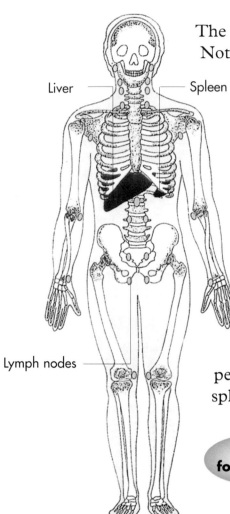

Liver

Spleen

Lymph nodes

Blood formation

The spleen is one of the main filters of the blood. Not only do the reticular cells remove the old and worn-out blood cells, but they will also remove any abnormal cells. This applies in particular to red blood cells, but white cells and platelets are also filtered selectively by the spleen when it is necessary.

The spleen will also remove abnormal particles that are floating in the bloodstream. It therefore plays a very important part in ridding the body of harmful bacteria.

In some circumstances, the spleen has a major role in the manufacture of new red blood cells. This does not happen in the normal adult but in people who have a bone marrow disease. The spleen and liver are major sites of red blood cell production. Another function of the spleen is to manufacture blood during gestation.

FACT FILE

The spleen is situated in the top left-hand corner of the abdomen, just below the diaphragm. It is in a relatively exposed position, which is why it is frequently damaged in accidents and has to be removed.

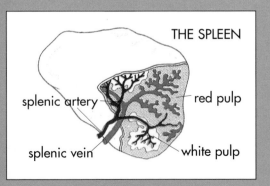

THE SPLEEN

splenic artery

red pulp

splenic vein

white pulp

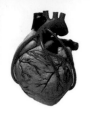

HOW ARE BLOOD TYPES DETERMINED?

Receptor	A	B	AB	O
Donor A				
B				
AB				
O				

Blood types are determined by the presence of antigens (a substance capable of stimulating an immune response) on the surfaces of the red cells. Although the red blood cells in different people look the same, they are, in fact, dissimilar. They can be divided into four main groups: A, B, AB, and O.

Blood can be transplanted from one person to another by what we call a blood transfusion. It is very important that the transfused blood matches the recipient's type. If the wrong types of blood are mixed together, serious blood clots can occur.

FACT FILE

Blood begins to clot as soon as it is exposed to the air, plugging the wound. White blood cells gather around the wound to kill invading microbes, and new skin cells grow into the healing wound beneath the scab.

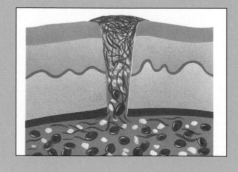

WHEN DO RED AND WHITE BLOOD CELLS DIE?

FACT FILE

An adult body has about 10 pints of blood. At any time, about 2.5 pints are in the arteries, 7 pints in the veins, and half a pint in the capillaries. The blood cells flow through a capillary for only half a second before they move into the small veins.

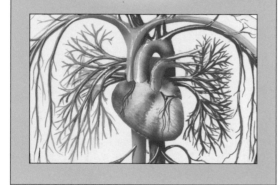

Both white and red blood cells are formed in the bone marrow. Each red blood cell measures about seven-thousandths of a millimeter in diameter and is shaped a little like a doughnut. They contain hemoglobin, which gives the cells their red pigment. There are 5 to 6 million red blood cells per cubic mm of blood. The red cell only survives about 120 days, and the damaged and old cells are removed by the spleen and liver.

A white blood cell is not really white, but is almost transparent. It can change shape, push out folds and finger-like projections, and move along by oozing and crawling like an amoeba in a pond. These cells survive less than a week.

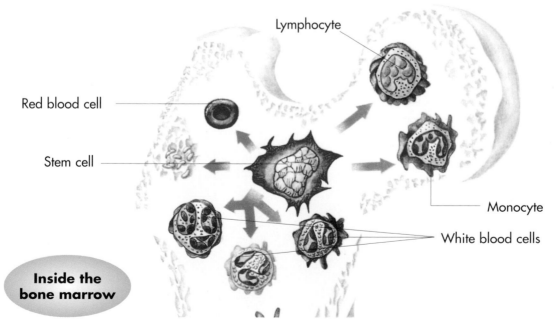

Lymphocyte

Red blood cell

Stem cell

Monocyte

White blood cells

Inside the bone marrow

ORGANS AND DIGESTION

CONTENTS

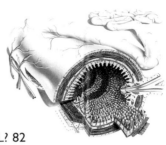

WHAT TRAVELS DOWN THE ALIMENTARY CANAL? 82
WHAT DOES THE THYROID GLAND DO? 83

HOW DO THE KIDNEYS WORK? 84
HOW DO THE KIDNEYS CONTROL BLOOD PRESSURE? 85

WHAT IS THE ROLE OF THE LIVER? 86
WHAT IS BILE? 87

WHERE DOES THE BODY STORE BILE? 88
WHERE DOES THE LIVER GET ITS BLOOD? 89

HOW DO WE DIGEST FOOD? 90
WHAT MAKES US HUNGRY? 91

WHAT IS THE PURPOSE OF OUR VOICE BOX? 92
WHY DO WE PRODUCE SALIVA? 93

WHAT IS INSIDE THE LUNGS? 94
WHAT IS BRONCHITIS? 95

WHAT IS INSULIN? 96
WHAT IS THE PANCREAS? 97

WHEN DOES FOOD REACH OUR INTESTINES? 98
HOW IS THE APPENDIX USED IN DIGESTION? 99

WHAT CAUSES THE LIVER TO STOP FUNCTIONING PROPERLY? 100
WHAT IS A CALORIE? 101

WHEN DOES RESPIRATION OCCUR? 102
WHY DO WE COUGH? 103

WHERE IS PAPILLAE FOUND? 104
WHERE IS THE EPIGLOTTIS FOUND? 105

WHERE ARE THE ALVEOLI LOCATED? 106
WHERE DOES THE EXCHANGE OF GASES TAKE PLACE? 107

WHERE DOES DIGESTION START? 108
WHERE IS THE DIGESTIVE PROCESS COMPLETED? 109

WHERE IS URINE STORED? 110
WHERE ARE NEPHRONS FOUND? 111

WHERE IS THE LARGEST GLAND IN THE BODY? 112
WHERE WOULD YOU USE A BRONCHOSCOPE? 113

WHY DO WE NEED VITAMIN C? 114
WHY ARE CARBOHYDRATES IMPORTANT? 115

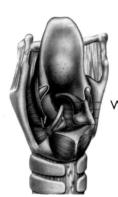

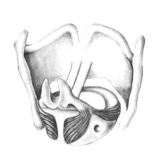

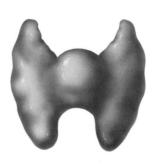

WHAT TRAVELS DOWN THE ALIMENTARY CANAL?

When human beings eat, the food is taken into the body and digested through a tube about 30 feet (9 m) long called the *alimentary canal*. Starting at the mouth, it includes the pharynx, esophagus, stomach, small and large intestines, and rectum.

When food is swallowed, the pharynx muscles force the food into the esophagus, where the muscles in its walls react with ebb-and-flow contractions known as peristalsis.

The food then moves down to the stomach as the lower esophageal sphincter relaxes, allowing digestion to take place.

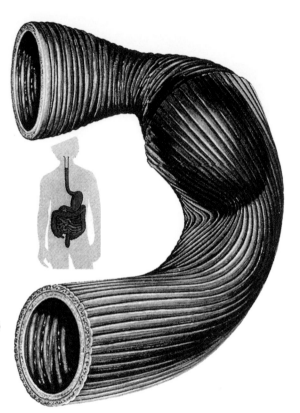

FACT FILE

The human esophagus is about 10 inches (25 cm) long. The length varies greatly in different animals. The esophagus of a fish is short, while that of a giraffe is extremely long. Many birds have a saclike part of the esophagus called the *crop* for temporary storage of food.

WHAT DOES THE THYROID GLAND DO?

The thyroid gland is an organ located in the front part of the neck. On each side of the windpipe, or trachea, is one of two lobes joined by a thin strip of tissue. A network of blood vessels is grouped around the gland. The function of the thyroid is to take iodine from the blood to make the active hormones thyroxine, also called *tetraiodothyronine* and *triiodothyronine*. Small chambers in the lobes, called *follicles*, store an inactive form of the thyroid hormones.

Thyroid hormones help regulate the body's cell metabolism. When they enter the bloodstream, the rate at which the blood cells convert oxygen and nutrients into energy and heat for the body's use is significantly increased. In children, thyroid hormones stimulate an increase in their growth rate. The release of thyroid hormones also helps stimulate mental activity and enhance the benefits of the other hormone-producing glands.

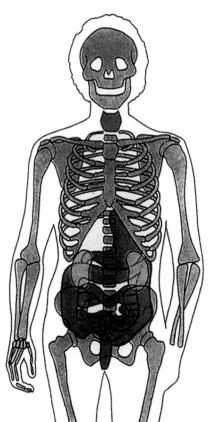

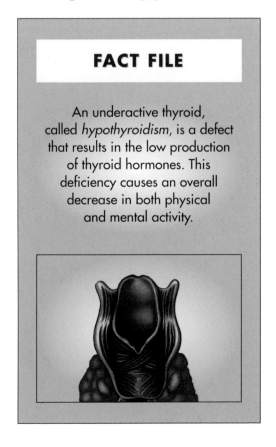

FACT FILE

An underactive thyroid, called *hypothyroidism*, is a defect that results in the low production of thyroid hormones. This deficiency causes an overall decrease in both physical and mental activity.

HOW DO THE KIDNEYS WORK?

Human kidneys are made up of three layers. On the outside of the organ, there is the cortex, then the medulla, and then the pelvis. Blood enters the medulla through the renal artery, which branches into smaller and smaller arteries, each of which finishes in a blood filtration unit called a *nephron*. Blood flows at high pressure through the capillaries of the Bowman's capsule (1), and only small molecules are forced through the walls (2) into the first part of the nephron (3). The filtrate passes down the proximal tubule, which secretes further metabolites and salts (4) and reabsorbs water, sodium, essential salts, glucose, and amino-acids into the blood (5). Unwanted salts, urea, and water are left as urine (6).

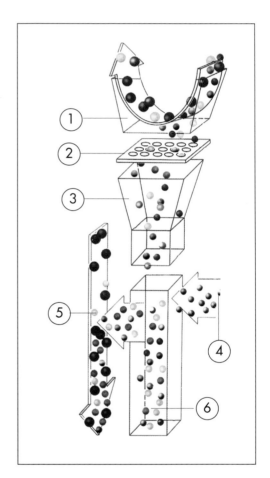

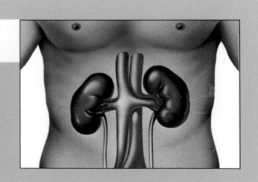

FACT FILE

Two healthy kidneys contain a total of about 2 million nephrons, which filter about 500 gallons (1900 liters) of blood daily.

How do the kidneys control blood pressure?

The kidneys help maintain the blood pressure of the body by releasing an enzyme called *renin*. The level of renin in the body depends upon the level of salt, which in turn is controlled by the action of the adrenal hormone, aldosterone, on the tubules. Renin activates another hormone, angiotensin. This has two effects: first, it constricts the arterioles and raises the blood pressure; second, it causes the adrenal gland to release aldosterone, making the kidneys retain salt and causing the blood pressure to rise.

The two kidneys perform many vital functions. The most important is the production of urine. But in addition to this, the kidneys secrete a hormone called *erythropoietin*, which controls the production of red blood cells. The kidneys convert vitamin D from an inactive to an active form. The active form is essential for normal bone development.

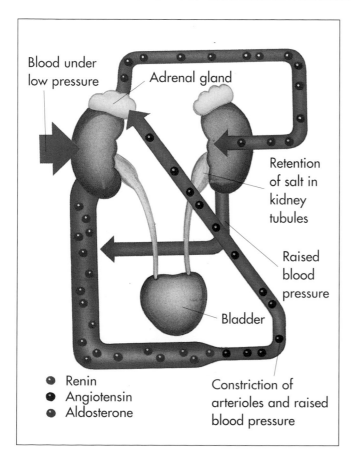

Blood under low pressure

Adrenal gland

Retention of salt in kidney tubules

Raised blood pressure

Bladder

- Renin
- Angiotensin
- Aldosterone

Constriction of arterioles and raised blood pressure

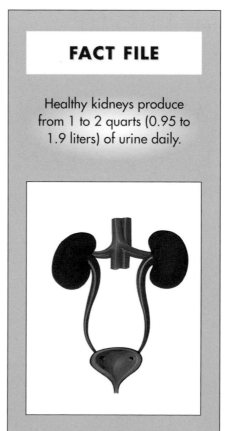

FACT FILE

Healthy kidneys produce from 1 to 2 quarts (0.95 to 1.9 liters) of urine daily.

WHAT IS THE ROLE OF THE LIVER?

The liver is one of the body's busiest organs. It does not squirm about or move, like the stomach, intestines, heart, or muscles. Its activities are invisible. The liver is the body's largest inner organ, weighing about 2 to 3 pounds, and fills the top part of the abdomen, especially on the right side. It has at least 500 known jobs in body chemistry, all different and important.

The liver has a special blood vessel–the hepatic portal vein. This does not come directly from the heart but carries blood that has been to the stomach, intestines, and spleen. This blood is rich in nutrients, which provide the body with its energy and raw materials. The liver processes many of the nutrients brought to it by the blood. It stores others, especially glucose sugar, minerals such as iron, and vitamins such as B12. It also detoxifies possible harmful substances.

Bile canaliculus

Hepatic cell

FACT FILE

Cirrhosis of the liver is an irreversible chronic disease characterized by the replacement of functioning liver tissue with bands and lumps of scar tissue. This disease is often associated with drinking too much alcohol.

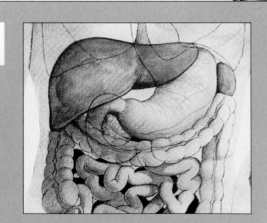

WHAT IS BILE?

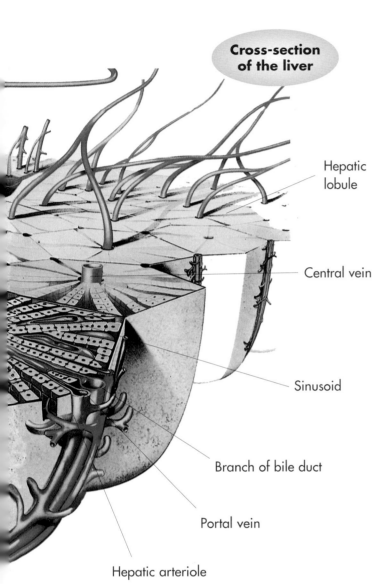

Cross-section of the liver

Hepatic lobule

Central vein

Sinusoid

Branch of bile duct

Portal vein

Hepatic arteriole

FACT FILE

Sometimes, the gall bladder gets filled with hard lumps, on average about the size of a pea. These are called *gallstones*. They are made from various substances, chiefly cholesterol and calcium, and can sometimes be removed by laser surgery.

On the right underside of the liver is the gall bladder. It is a small bag that contains a yellowish fluid called *bile*. Bile is a solution of cholesterol, bile salts, and pigments. The liver produces up to a full quart of bile every day. Some of this stays in the liver and some in the gall bladder, until you have a meal. Then, bile flows from the gall bladder and liver to a main tube, called the *common bile duct*, which empties into the small intestine. Bile is a waste product from the liver, but it also helps with digestion. The mineral salts in it break up, or emulsify, fatty foods in the intestine by turning the fats into tiny droplets.

WHERE DOES THE BODY STORE BILE?

Bile is stored in a small pouch called the *gallbladder*, an oval sac located underneath the right part of the liver. At any one time, it can hold about 1½ fluid ounces (44 ml) of bile. The neck of the gallbladder is joined to the cystic duct, which in turn enters the hepatic duct, a tube from the liver. The two tubes make up the common bile duct.

When food is being digested, bile flows from the liver into the common bile duct via the hepatic duct. Then, it empties into the duodenum, the first part of the small intestine. When food is not being eaten, the bile still flows from the liver into the common bile duct even though it is not needed. Prevented from entering the duodenum by a tiny, ring-shaped muscle called the *sphincter of Oddi*, which tightens around the opening, the fluid is routed into the gallbladder to be concentrated and retained until required for the digestive process.

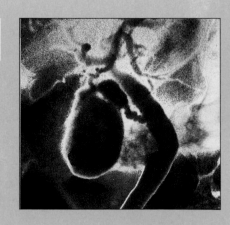

Liver

Gallbladder

FACT FILE

Sometimes, the gallbladder gets filled with hard lumps, on average about the size of a pea. They are made from various substances, mainly cholesterol and calcium. They can be removed by surgery or smashed into tiny pieces by very high-pitched sound waves called *ultrasound*.

WHERE DOES THE LIVER GET ITS BLOOD?

The main functions of the liver are helping the body digest and utilize food and purifying the blood of poisons and waste. But the liver probably does more jobs than any other organ in the body. The liver has an unusual blood supply system. Like other organs, the liver receives blood containing oxygen from the heart. This blood enters the liver through the hepatic artery. The liver also receives blood filled with nutrients, or digested food particles, from the small intestine. This blood enters the liver through the portal vein. In the liver, the hepatic artery and the portal vein branch into a network of tiny blood vessels that empty into the sinusoids.

The liver cells absorb nutrients and oxygen from the blood as it flows through the sinusoids. They also filter out wastes and poisons. At the same time, they secrete sugar, vitamins, minerals, and other substances into the blood. The sinusoids drain into the central veins, which join to form the hepatic vein. Blood leaves the liver through the hepatic vein.

Stomach

Spleen

FACT FILE

The liver plays an essential role in the storage of certain vitamins. The liver stores vitamin A, as well as vitamins D, E, and K, and those of the B-complex group. It also stores iron and other minerals.

HOW DO WE DIGEST FOOD?

In order to keep us alive and healthy, the food we eat must be broken down and utilized in a process we call *digestion*. In the mouth, saliva helps break down starches. When food has been moistened and crushed in the mouth, it travels to the stomach. Here, the juices from the stomach wall are mixed with the food, helping to break down proteins into simpler forms to aid digestion. The starches continue to break down until the material in the stomach becomes too acid.

The materials in the stomach are churned about to mix the digestive juices well throughout the food. When the food becomes liquified, it enters the small intestine. In the first part of the small intestine, the duodenum, digestion continues. Juices from the pancreas and liver help to further break down the foods. The breakdown of proteins and starch digestion is finished here. Fats are split into finer parts. It is also in the small intestine that digested food is absorbed into the blood and lymph. Finally, in the large intestine, water is absorbed, and the contents become more solid, so they can leave the body as waste material.

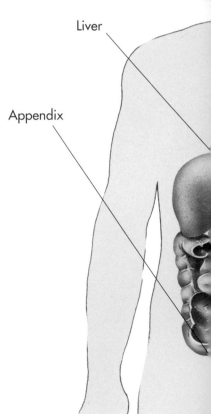

Liver

Appendix

FACT FILE

Cholesterol is a fatty substance found in blood and some fatty foods. It can be deposited on the walls of arteries, making them more narrow. This reduces blood flow in the arteries and can cause blockages.

Build up of cholesterol

Artery wall

WHAT MAKES US HUNGRY?

We all know that we need food regularly. When we don't get it, our body tells us by making us feel hungry. But how does our mind get the message to tell us we feel hungry? Surprisingly, hunger is not directly related to an empty stomach. It starts because certain nutritive elements are missing in the blood, and when the blood vessels sense this defecit, they send a message to an area of the brain we call the *lateral hypothalamus*, or "hunger center." The hunger center works on the stomach and intestine like a car's accelerator. While the blood has sufficient nutrition, the hunger center slows up activity in the stomach and the intestine, but when the food is missing, it makes them more active. This being the reason that we often hear our stomach "growling" when we are hungry.

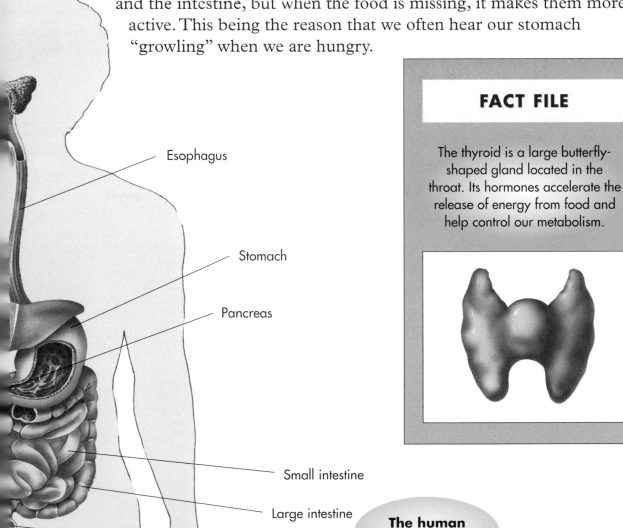

Esophagus

Stomach

Pancreas

Small intestine

Large intestine

Rectum

The human digestive system

FACT FILE

The thyroid is a large butterfly-shaped gland located in the throat. Its hormones accelerate the release of energy from food and help control our metabolism.

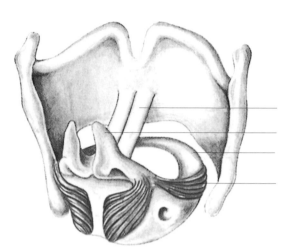

Posterior view of larynx

Speech and voice mechanism

Vocal cords closed

Arytenoid cartilage

Cricoid cartilage

Laryngeal muscles

Side view of larynx

WHAT IS THE PURPOSE OF OUR VOICE BOX?

When air is forced through our vocal cords, they vibrate, making a sound. The vocal cords are two rubbery bands of cartilage inside the larynx. This body part is called the *voice box*. It is at the top of the windpipe.

The muscles of the larynx can alter the shape of the cords to produce different sounds. The cords produce low-pitched sounds when they are close together and high-pitched sounds when they are far apart. The harder the air is forced out, the louder the sounds become. You use the muscles of your throat, mouth, and lips to form the sounds into words.

FACT FILE

At the age of puberty, a boy's voice "breaks." The larynx enlarges due to the effect of the male hormone, testosterone, and the vocal cords become longer. This means that the boy now has a lower bass range.

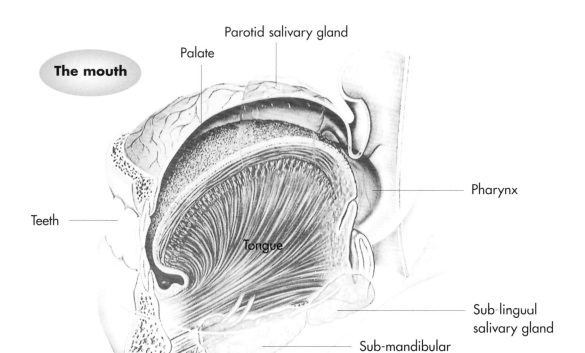

The mouth

Palate

Parotid salivary gland

Teeth

Tongue

Pharynx

Sub-linguul salivary gland

Sub-mandibular salivary gland

WHY DO WE PRODUCE SALIVA?

The major function of saliva is to help in the process of digestion. It keeps the mouth moist and comfortable when we eat and helps to moisten dry food, allowing it to be chewed and swallowed more easily. The mucus in saliva coats the chewed food and acts as a lubricant to help us to swallow.

The enzyme ptyalin, which is found in saliva, begins the first stage of digestion. It begins to break down starchy food into simpler sugars. Saliva also allows us to taste our food and drink. Each day we all usually produce about 3 pints (1.7 liters) of saliva.

FACT FILE

You can check where you experience the four tastes by dabbing your tongue with a little salt, sugar, coffee grounds (bitter), and lemon juice (sour).

WHAT IS INSIDE THE LUNGS?

Every human being has two lungs, one in each side of the chest, enclosed by an airtight box. The ribs, the muscles that join them, and a tough sheet of muscle called the *diaphragm* form this box. The lungs are spongy organs made up of tightly packed tissue, nerves, and blood vessels. In order to get the maximum surface area, the inside of the lungs is made up of tiny air sacs called *alveoli*, which are surrounded by capillaries. The walls of the alveoli and capillaries are so thin that oxygen and carbon dioxide can pass through them. The alveoli of an adult have a total surface area of 750 sq. ft. (70 m2). The whole breathing apparatus is designed to bring fresh air as close as possible to the blood. When you breathe in, the diaphragm pulls down so that your lungs expand and fill with air. When you breathe out, your diaphragm relaxes, your lungs shrink and expel some of the air in them.

The alveolar sac

Alveolar walls

Connective tissue

Alveolar lining

FACT FILE

Underwater animals, like fish, have breathing organs called *gills* instead of lungs. Gills can take in oxygen from the water. To enable us to breathe underwater, we need an oxygen tank. If our lungs filled with water, we would drown.

WHAT IS BRONCHITIS?

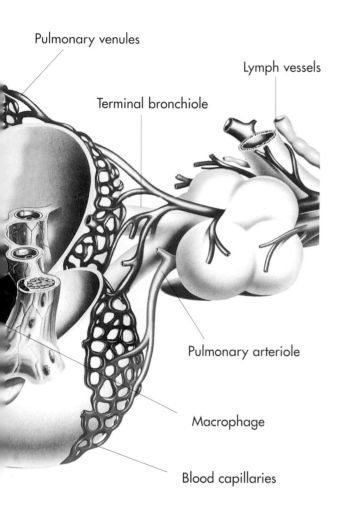

Pulmonary venules

Lymph vessels

Terminal bronchiole

Pulmonary arteriole

Macrophage

Blood capillaries

FACT FILE

Smoking damages the natural cleaning mechanism of the lungs and also poisons the cells that line the lungs. Regular smokers often suffer from bronchitis.

Bronchitis is an inflammation of all or part of the bronchial tree (the bronchi), through which air passes into the lungs. During the passage through the bronchi, microorganisms and other foreign bodies are removed from the air by tiny hairlike structures called *cilia*, which project from the cells that line the bronchial wall. These cilia have a wavelike motion and sweep the foreign material upward toward the trachea and larynx. Because of this irritation, a thick mucus is produced by glands in the bronchial wall and aid in the elimination of the foreign material. The secreted mucus stimulate nerve endings in the bronchial wall and cause you to cough in an effort to expel the foreign material.

Acute bronchitis is most frequently caused by viruses responsible for upper respiratory infections. Often these are caused by the common cold.

WHAT IS INSULIN?

Insulin is a hormone produced by the pancreas. The purpose of insulin is to keep the level of sugar in the blood down to normal levels.

If the level of sugar in the blood begins to rise above certain limits, the Islets of Langerhans respond by releasing insulin into the bloodstream. The insulin then acts to oppose the effects of hormones, such as cortisone and adrenalin, both of which raise the level of sugar in the blood. The insulin exerts its effect by allowing sugar to pass from the bloodstream into the body's cells to be used as a fuel.

FACT FILE

When a doctor replaces a damaged organ with a healthy one from a donor, the operation is called a *transplant*. The heart, liver, kidneys, and lungs can all be transplanted.

Cross-section of a kidney

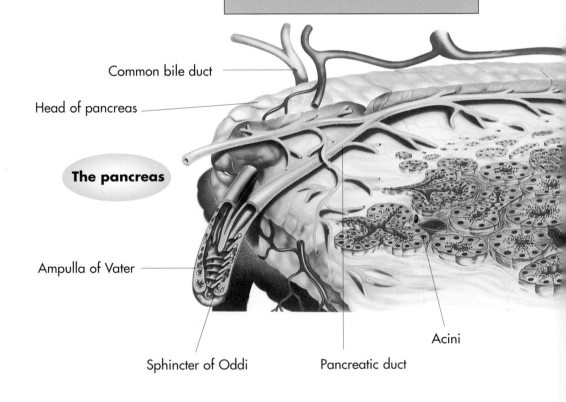

Common bile duct

Head of pancreas

The pancreas

Ampulla of Vater

Sphincter of Oddi

Pancreatic duct

Acini

WHAT IS THE PANCREAS?

FACT FILE

Are you frightened of spiders? When you're frightened or angry, your brain tells its hypothalamus area to send messages to your adrenal glands, which produce two "emergency" hormones called *adrenalin* and *noradrenalin*.

The pancreas is one of the largest glands in the body and is really two glands in one. Almost all of its cells are concerned with secretion. The pancreas lies across the upper part of the abdomen in front of the spine and on top of the aorta and the vena cava (the body's main artery and vein). The duodenum is wrapped around the head of the pancreas. The basic structures in the pancreas are the acini, which are collections of secreting cells around the end of a small duct. Each duct joins with ducts from other acini until all of them eventually connect with the main duct running down the middle of the pancreas. The Islets of Langerhans are cells that are responsible for the secretion of insulin, which is needed by the body for the constant control of its sugar level. The Islets also produce a hormone called *glucagon*, which raises the level of sugar in the blood. The pancreas also plays an important part in digestion as it secretes digestive enzymes into the small intestine.

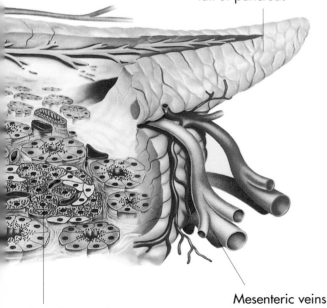

Tail of pancreas

Mesenteric veins

Islets of Langerhans

WHEN DOES FOOD REACH OUR INTESTINES?

Everything you eat has to be broken down before the nutrients in it can be absorbed by your body to make energy. This takes place in your digestive system. The food leaves your stomach a little at a time and goes into your small intestine. This is where most of the digestion takes place by adding digestive chemicals and absorbing the digested nutrients into the body. The lining of the intestine is folded into millions of tiny fingers called *villi*. Undigested food continues its journey on to the large intestine where excess water and minerals are extracted from the leftover food.

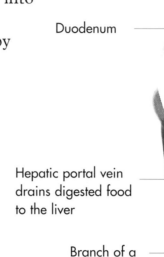

Duodenum

Hepatic portal vein drains digested food to the liver

Branch of a mesenteric artery

Muscle layers

Enzyme-producing glands

FACT FILE

How much energy do you use?

Sitting: 43–72 calories per hour
Walking: 144–216 calories per hour
Running: 432–575 calories per hour

HOW IS THE APPENDIX USED IN DIGESTION?

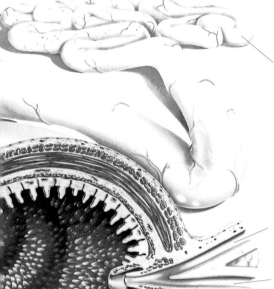

Jejunum and ileum are two subdivisions of the small intestine.

Common bile duct

Pancreatic duct

Villi are finger-like projections lining the small intestine.

The appendix is a narrow tube-like piece of gut resembling a tail. It is located at the end of the large intestine. The tip of the tube is closed; the other end joins on to the large intestine. It is only found in human beings, certain species of apes, and in the wombat.

Other animals have an organ in the same position as the appendix that acts as an additional stomach. This is where the fibrous part of plants and cellulose is digested by bacteria. It seems that as we evolved through the ages and began to eat less cellulose instead of meat, a special organ was no longer needed for its digestion.

FACT FILE

The only time we are aware of the appendix is when it becomes infected. This is known as appendicitis. For the most part, it is a useless part of the large intestine with no known function.

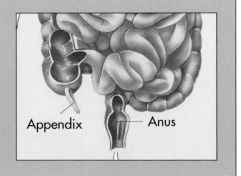

Appendix   Anus

WHAT CAUSES THE LIVER TO STOP FUNCTIONING PROPERLY?

The liver has two vital roles to play: making or processing new chemicals and neutralizing poisons and waste products. The liver is the largest organ in the body, weighing around 4 lb (1.36 and 1.81 kg). It is only possible for the blood to get back to the heart and lungs from the stomach by first passing through a system of veins in the liver, known as the portal system.

A variety of things, including viruses, drugs, environmental pollutants, genetic disorders, and systemic diseases, can cause the liver to stop functioning properly. However, the liver has a marvelous capacity to renew itself and will usually return to normal once the causes are removed or eliminated.

FACT FILE

If the kidneys do not work properly, they can become "furred" up with hard crusts and crystals of chemicals from the urine. These deposits are called *kidney stones*. They can be removed by an operation, dissolved by drugs, or shattered into tiny fragments by high-energy ultrasonic sound waves.

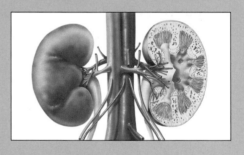

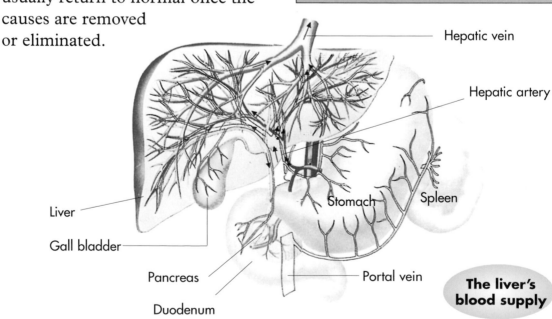

Hepatic vein

Hepatic artery

Liver

Gall bladder

Pancreas

Duodenum

Stomach

Spleen

Portal vein

The liver's blood supply

WHAT IS A CALORIE?

230 calories per slice

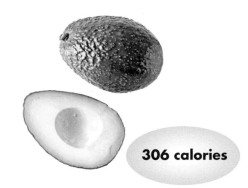

306 calories

A calorie is a measurement of energy or heat. One calorie is the amount of heat it takes to raise the temperature of one gram of water one degree. But what does this have to do with food? Well, we eat food to supply us with energy, and so energy in foods is measured in calories. When goods are metabolized or utilized by being combined with oxygen in the body cells, they give off calories (or energy). In measuring the energy value of food, we use the "large" or kilogram calorie, which equals one thousand regular calories. Each type of food furnishes a certain number of calories. For instance, one gram of protein provides four calories, but one gram of fat provides nine calories. The amount of calories the body needs depends on the work the body has to do.

190 calories

FACT FILE

The body uses up what calories it needs and stores some of them for future use. The body can store about one-third of the amount it needs each day. The rest becomes fat!

WHEN DOES RESPIRATION OCCUR?

FACT FILE

The average person at rest breathes in and out about 10–14 times per minute. If you sing or play an instrument like a trumpet, you need lots of breath.

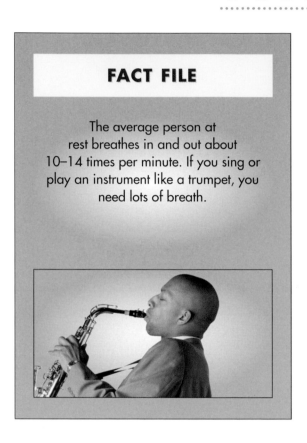

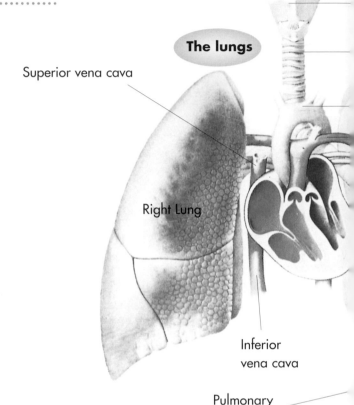

The lungs

Superior vena cava

Right Lung

Inferior vena cava

Pulmonary venule

Respiration occurs when you draw air in through the nose and mouth and into the lungs. Like all movements in the body, those of respiration rely on muscle power. There are two main sets of breathing muscles: the intercostal muscle and the diaphragm. Breathe in deeply and watch your ribs rise and your chest expand. Together, these muscles make the chest bigger and stretch the spongy lungs inside. As the lungs enlarge, they suck air down the windpipe. This is how we breathe in. Then the muscles relax. The ribs fall back down, and the diaphragm resumes its domed shape as the spongy, elastic lungs spring back to their smaller size. The lungs blow some of their air up the windpipe. This is how we breathe out.

The movements of breathing are controlled by the brain. It sends out signals to make the muscles contract. The signals pass along nerves to the intercostal and diaphragm muscles, making them contract. This happens every few seconds, even when you are asleep.

WHY DO WE COUGH?

Larynx

Trachea

Aorta

Pulmonary artery

Left main bronchus

Small bronchus

Terminal bronchiole

Coughing is the way in which the lungs dislodge anything that blocks the air passages. Usually, these are only minor blockages caused by a build-up of mucus when you have a cold or chest infection. When you cough, your vocal cords press together to seal off the air passages. At the same time, your chest muscles become tense, raising the pressure in your lungs. When you release the air, it rushes out, carrying the obstruction with it.

The delicate alveoli inside the lungs can be damaged by many different things, thus causing us to cough. One is tobacco smoke, which clogs the alveoli and airways with thick tar. Others are the polluting gases that hover in the air of many big cities, coming from vehicle exhausts as well as factory and power-plant chimneys. Some types of industrial dust and particles floating in the air, such as asbestos or coal-mine dust, can cause considerable damage to the lungs.

FACT FILE

It can be quite hard to breathe when you are at the top of a mountain. At high altitudes, the air is thinner so there is not as much oxygen in it. This means that you will breathe heavily if you exert yourself.

WHERE IS PAPILLAE FOUND?

FACT FILE

The sense of taste is the crudest of our five senses. It is limited in both range and versatility. Each papilla contains one to two hundred taste buds.

Papillae can be found on the surface of your tongue. As well as being an important aid in chewing and swallowing and in the formation of sounds when we speak, the tongue is the main taste organ. Covered with a mucous membrane, the underside of the tongue is smooth. The top of the tongue feels rough because of many papillae (small projections). The four types of papillae are filiform, folioform, vallate, (all at the back of the tongue), and fungiform. The papillae hold four types of taste buds to distinguish between sweet, sour, salty, and bitter tastes.

Epiglottis

Filiform papillae

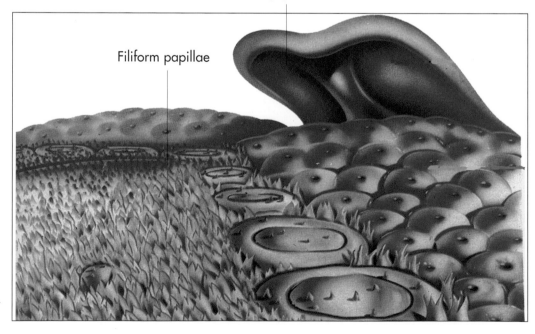

WHERE IS THE EPIGLOTTIS FOUND?

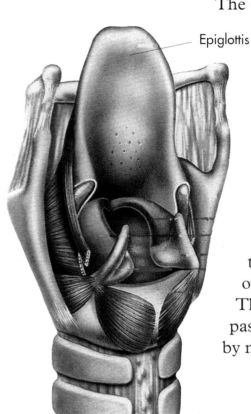

Epiglottis

The epiglottis is found in the throat. The term *throat* refers to the area located in the neck at the front of the backbone. It houses a variety of structures, all important in eating and breathing, including the pharynx, the larynx, part of the trachea, and part of the esophagus.

To allow a person to swallow, the air passage has to be blocked off. The opening to the nose is closed by the soft palate pressing against the back of the pharynx. The larynx, covered by an oval-shaped lid called the *epiglottis*, rises. This directs the food into the correct passage, the esophagus, and is then carried by muscular waves into the stomach.

FACT FILE

The thyroid is shaped like a bow tie under the skin of the neck. It manufactures three main hormones: calcitonin—which controls the level of calcium minerals in the blood and bones; and thyroxine and tri-iodothyronine—which affect blood pressure and the speed of general body chemistry.

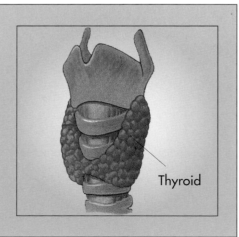

Thyroid

WHERE ARE THE ALVEOLI LOCATED?

With a sponge-like texture, the lungs are rather like flexible bags, filled with millions of minute air chambers called *alveoli*. The area surface of the walls of these aveoli is the equivalent to half a tennis court!

Hanging inside the rib cage, the lungs are suspended from above the first rib down to the diaphragm, which is a sheet of muscle separating the chest cavity from the abdomen. The outer surface of the lungs is covered by a strong, thin membrane called the *visceral pleura*. Between the two lungs is the esophagus tube, which connects the mouth and the stomach and the large blood vessels and the heart.

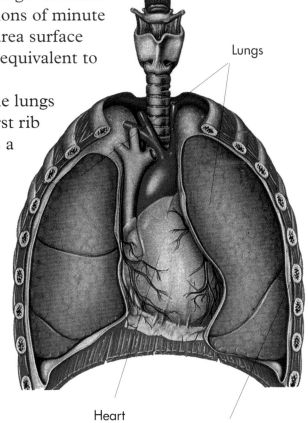

Lungs

Heart

Rib cage

FACT FILE

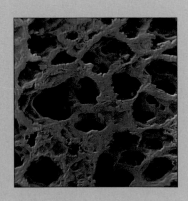

Each alveolar duct in the lungs supplies about 20 alveoli. The very thin walls of each alveolus contain networks of extremely small blood vessels called *pulmonary capillaries*. Gas is exchanged between the blood in these capillaries and the gas in the alveoli.

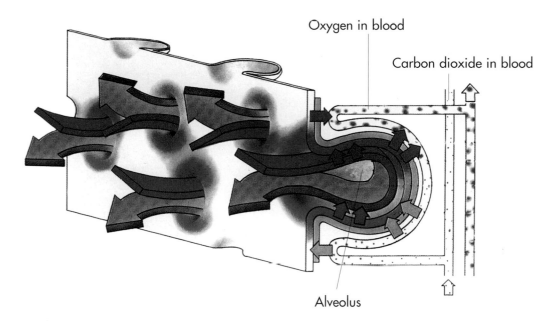

Oxygen in blood

Carbon dioxide in blood

Alveolus

WHERE DOES THE EXCHANGE OF GASES TAKE PLACE?

The exchange of gases takes place within the respiratory system. The primary function of the respiratory system is to supply the blood with oxygen in order for the blood to deliver oxygen to all parts of the body. Breathing enables the respiratory system to do this. When we breathe, we inhale oxygen and exhale carbon dioxide. This is known as the exchange of gases and is the body's means of getting oxygen to the blood. Oxygen enters the respiratory system through the mouth and the nose. It is the job of the diaphragm to help pump the carbon dioxide out of the lungs and pull the oxygen into the lungs. The diaphragm is a sheet of muscles that lies across the bottom of the chest cavity.

FACT FILE

Inspired air contains 20 percent oxygen, 0.03 percent carbon dioxide, and the rest is nitrogen. Expired air contains 16 percent oxygen, and the carbon dioxide is increased to 4 percent.

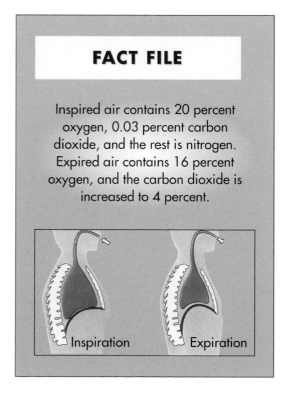

Inspiration

Expiration

WHERE DOES DIGESTION START?

Digestion starts in the mouth. Chewing is important to good digestion for two reasons. When chewed food is ground into fine particles, the digestive juices can act more easily. As the food is chewed, it is moistened and mixed with saliva, which contains the enzyme ptyalin. Ptyalin changes some of the starches in the food to sugar. After the food is swallowed, it passes through the esophagus into the stomach. The digestive juice in the stomach is called *gastric juice*. It contains hydrochloric acid and the enzyme pepsin. This juice begins the digestion of protein foods, such as meat, eggs, and milk. Starches, sugars, and fats are not digested by the gastric juice. After a meal, some food remains in the stomach for two to five hours.

FACT FILE

Almost no digestion occurs in the large intestine. It stores waste food products and absorbs water and small amounts of minerals. The waste that accumulates in the large intestine is roughage that cannot be digested.

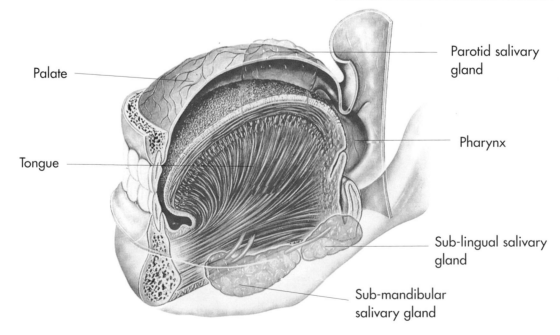

Palate

Tongue

Parotid salivary gland

Pharynx

Sub-lingual salivary gland

Sub-mandibular salivary gland

WHERE IS THE DIGESTIVE PROCESS COMPLETED?

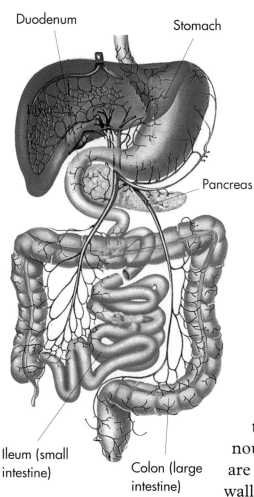

Duodenum

Stomach

Liver

Pancreas

Ileum (small intestine)

Colon (large intestine)

In the small intestine, the digestive process is completed on partly digested food by pancreatic juice, intestinal juice, and bile. The pancreatic juice is produced by the pancreas and pours into the small intestine through a tube, or duct. The intestinal juice is produced by the walls of the small intestine. It has milder digestive effects than the pancreatic juice but carries out similar digestion. Bile is produced in the liver, stored in the gallbladder, and flows into the small intestine through the bile duct. When the food is completely digested, it is absorbed by tiny blood and lymph vessels in the walls of the small intestine. It is then carried into the circulation for nourishment of the body. Food particles are small enough to pass through the walls of the intestine and blood vessels only when they are completely digested.

FACT FILE

The small intestine is about 7.6 yards (7 m) long and is lined with small finger-like protuberances called *villi*. The successful absorption of nutrients depends on their transport away from the cells of the villi into the bloodstream.

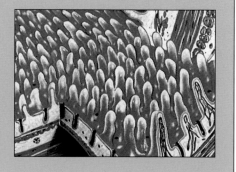

WHERE IS URINE STORED?

The urinary bladder is a muscular organ where urine is stored before being expelled from the body. In human beings and many other mammals, the process of emptying the bladder is controlled voluntarily. Urine is contually being drained from the kidneys into the bladder, which lies just behind the pubis bone in the pelvis, via two tubes called *ureters*. At the neck of the bladder is the uretha, a wider tube which leads out of the body, and through which the urine passes when it leaves the bladder. To prevent urine from constantly flowing out of the bladder, a complex ring of muscles called the *urethral sphincter* surround the bladder neck.

FACT FILE

We lose around 5 pints (3 liters) of water a day as sweat, breath, and urine. We also get rid of extra salt in sweat and expel waste carbon dioxide gas when we breathe out.

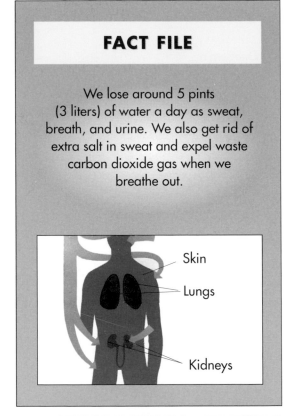

Skin

Lungs

Kidneys

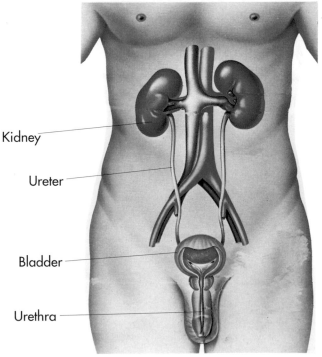

Kidney

Ureter

Bladder

Urethra

WHERE ARE NEPHRONS FOUND?

Nephrons are found in the kidneys; they are millions of tiny filtering units. The renal artery brings unfiltered blood to the kidneys. It branches into over 1 million capillaries inside each kidney. Each capillary is twisted into a knot called the *glomerulus*, which is enclosed by a structure called a *Bowman's capsule*. Blood is cleaned as it filters through the capsule and the tubule attached to it. Clean blood passes back into the capillaries, which join up into the renal vein. Urine continues down the tubule, which joins up with other tubules to form the ureter leading to the bladder.

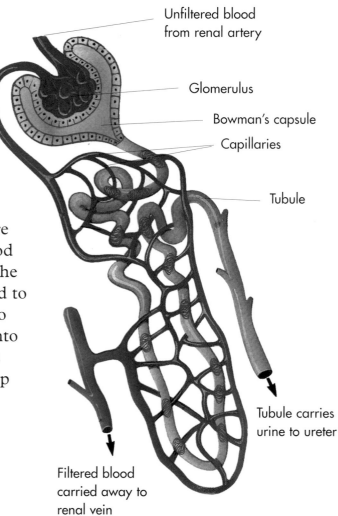

Unfiltered blood from renal artery

Glomerulus

Bowman's capsule

Capillaries

Tubule

Tubule carries urine to ureter

Filtered blood carried away to renal vein

FACT FILE

The two kidneys perform many vital functions, of which the most important is the production of urine. Two healthy kidneys contain a total of about 2 million nephrons, which filter about 500 gallons (1900 liters) of blood daily.

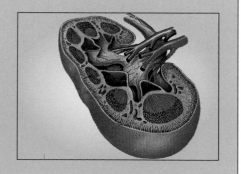

WHERE IS THE LARGEST GLAND IN THE BODY?

The liver is the largest and one of the most complex of human beings' organs. It functions as the body's main chemical processing plant and food storehouse. Located under the diaphragm and above the stomach and intestines in the upper-right part of the abdomen, the liver is a reddish-brown mass that weighs about 3 pounds (1.4 kg). One of the many essential functions it performs is that of helping the body to digest food. The liver produces and discharges *bile*, a digestive fluid. Extra supplies of bile are stored in the gallbladder, a pear-shaped pouch that lies just under the liver. The greenish-yellow bile then travels from the liver to the small intestine, where it helps digest fats.

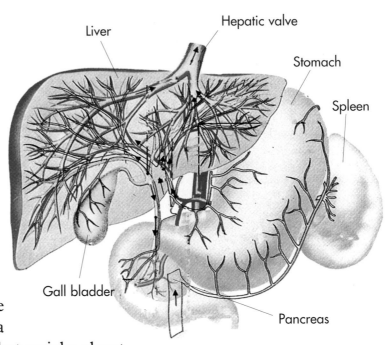

Liver · Hepatic valve · Stomach · Spleen · Gall bladder · Pancreas

FACT FILE

The liver has a remarkable ability to produce new cells to replace its own diseased or damaged cells. For example, surgeons can remove a section of a healthy liver from an adult and transplant it into a child who has a diseased liver. The child's new liver will grow as the child grows.

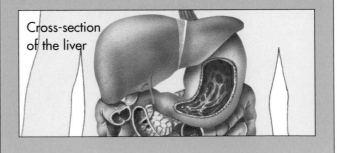

Cross-section of the liver

WHERE WOULD YOU USE A BRONCHOSCOPE?

A bronchoscope is an instrument that consists of an arrangement of lights and mirrors within a hollow tube, which is used to examine the trache and the lungs' bronchial tubes.

The apparatus allows doctors to observe potentially diseased arcas that cannot be detected by X-rays by inserting instruments through the patient's mouth or nose into the throat and lungs. In addition, doctors and surgeons can use them to remove small tumors, foreign matter, and samples of tissue by means of attachments such as a forceps, sucking needlc, or brush.

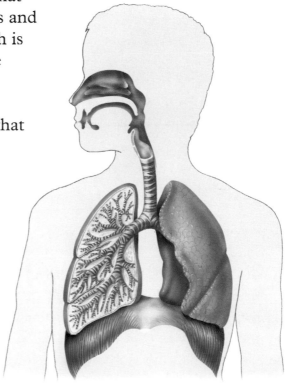

FACT FILE

Because the lungs must inhale the air from the environment, they are exposed to bacteria, viruses, dust, and pollutants that are mixed with the air. A sticky fluid called *mucus* lines the airways and traps most of these foreign substances.

WHY DO WE NEED VITAMIN C?

The food we take into our bodies supplies us with many important substances such as proteins, fats, carbohydrates, water, and mineral substances. But these alone are not enough. In order to maintain life, we need other substances known as vitamins. Vitamin C can be found in citrus fruits and fresh vegetables. When there is a lack of vitamins in our body, diseases can occur. What actually happens when there is a lack of Vitamin C in the body? The blood vessels become fragile and bleed easily. Black-and-blue marks appear on the skin and near the eyes. The gums bleed easily. Our hormones and enzymes do not function well, and our resistance to infection by bacteria is lowered.

Long before human beings knew about vitamins, people observed that if they couldn't get certain types of foods, diseases would develop. Sailors, for instance, who went on long trips and couldn't get fresh vegetables, would develop a disease called *scurvy*. In the seventeenth century, British sailors were given lemons and limes to help prevent this disease.

FACT FILE

Fruits contain energy and a wide range of essential vitamins and minerals. Vitamins are chemicals that we need to stay healthy. Some are stored in the body, and others need to be eaten every day.

WHY ARE CARBOHYDRATES IMPORTANT?

Human beings need a certain amount of food each day to give them energy. Almost all foods supply some energy, but carbohydrates give us the most. Carbohydrates include foods like bread, cereal, potatoes, rice, and pasta. Our bodies have other requirements as well. In order to make sure that we are taking in everything we need, we should eat a wide variety of foods, with the correct amounts of carbohydrates, fat, and protein. A diet which fulfills these requirements is called a *balanced* diet. These food groups serve different purposes: carbohydrates for energy and protein to build and repair cells, and to keep our bones, muscles, blood, and skin healthy.

FACT FILE

Bananas are a good source of energy because the body absorbs them quickly. Ripe bananas give off a gas that causes other fruit to ripen rapidly and then rot.

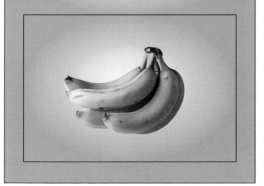

BRAIN AND

NERVOUS SYSTEM

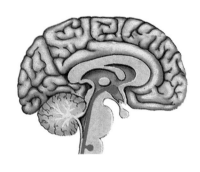

CONTENTS

WHAT IS THE AUTONOMIC NERVOUS SYSTEM? 118
HOW DO NERVE IMPULSES WORK? 119

HOW ARE MESSAGES PASSED THROUGH THE NERVOUS SYSTEM? 120
HOW DOES THE BRAIN WORK? 121

HOW DOES MEMORY WORK? 122
WHEN DO WE SUFFER FROM REFERRED PAIN? 123

WHAT ARE THE AREAS OF THE BRAIN CALLED? 124
WHAT ARE THE THREE MAIN FUNCTIONS OF THE BRAIN? 125

WHAT CONTROLS OUR BALANCE? 126
WHAT CONTROLS OUR TEMPERATURE? 127

WHEN DOES OUR SENSE OF TOUCH ALERT THE BRAIN OF DANGER? 128
WHEN DO WE USE OUR BRAIN TO SMELL? 129

WHERE IS SEROTONIN PRODUCED? 130
WHERE IS THE CEREBRUM? 131

WHY DO WE DREAM? 132
WHY DO WE AWAKEN FROM SLEEP? 133

WHY DO WE GET THIRSTY? 134
WHY DO WE GET HUNGRY? 135

WHY ARE SOME PEOPLE LEFT-HANDED? 136
WHY CAN WE BALANCE ON TWO LEGS? 137

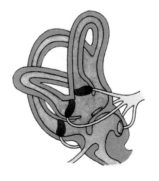

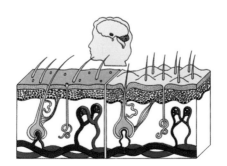

WHAT IS THE AUTONOMIC NERVOUS SYSTEM?

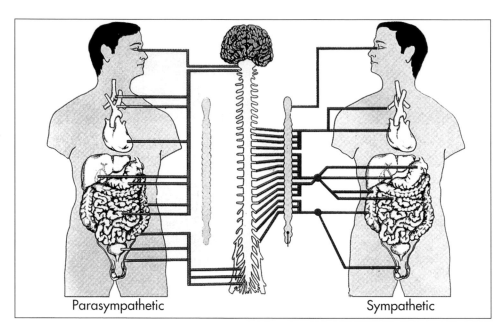

Parasympathetic   Sympathetic

There are many processes, such as breathing and digestion, that would be impossible for the body to regulate by conscious control from the brain. In order that these can function "automatically," we have what is called an *autonomic nervous system*, which consists of two elements, the *sympathetic* and the *parasympathetic* system. The parasympathetic nerves make the body calm and relaxed, and slow down processes such as digestion and heartbeat. The sympathetic nerves speed up all these processes and activities so that the body is ready to spring into action. Between these two nerve sets, the body's internal conditions are fine-tuned.

FACT FILE

The whole autonomic system is controlled by an area of the brain called the *hypothalamus*. This receives information about any variations in the body.

HOW DO NERVE IMPULSES WORK?

A nerve impulse is like a simple message: it is either on or off. Because there are so many neurons which are connected to one another, this simple signal is enough to carry the most complicated messages throughout the body's whole nervous system. As a nerve impulse arrives at the junction between two nerve cells, it is carried across the gap, or synapse, by chemicals called *neurotransmitters*. These contact sensitive areas in the next nerve cell, and the nerve impulse is carried along.

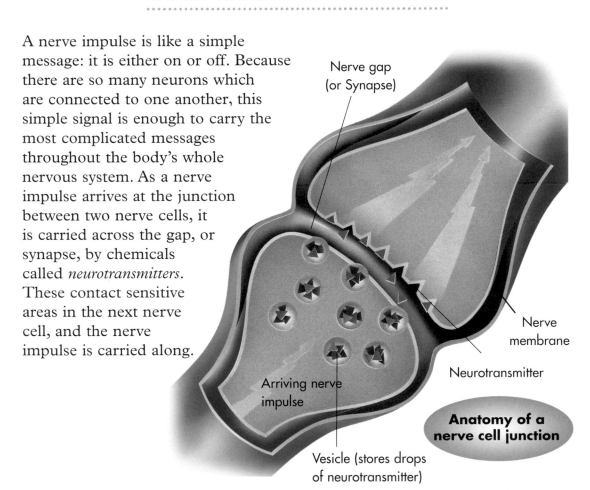

Nerve gap (or Synapse)

Nerve membrane

Neurotransmitter

Arriving nerve impulse

Anatomy of a nerve cell junction

Vesicle (stores drops of neurotransmitter)

FACT FILE

Scientists have produced maps showing how electrical activity in one part of the brain can cause a movement or other reaction. This mapping has been done during brain surgery. Because there are no sense organs in the brain, it is possible to operate on people who are fully conscious, without them feeling any pain. This enables doctors to know which part of the brain has been damaged after an accident.

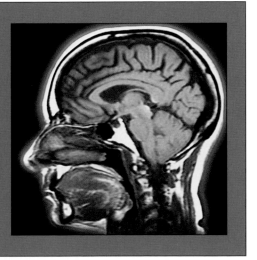

HOW ARE MESSAGES PASSED THROUGH THE NERVOUS SYSTEM?

Nerve impulses that pass through the nervous system are able to jump from one neuron to the next. Inside the nerve fiber, the nerve impulse travels like an electrical signal. When it reaches the end of the long fiber, it jumps across to the next neuron by means of a chemical transmitter. This chemical is released from the branched ends of the fiber. As this transmitter substance contacts the next neuron, it starts another nerve impulse. This whole process is very fast, with nerve impulses traveling along the largest nerve fibers at 295 feet per second.

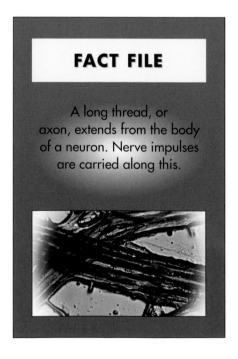

FACT FILE

A long thread, or axon, extends from the body of a neuron. Nerve impulses are carried along this.

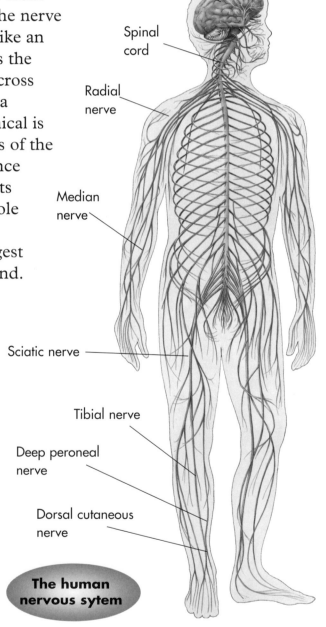

Brain

Spinal cord

Radial nerve

Median nerve

Sciatic nerve

Tibial nerve

Deep peroneal nerve

Dorsal cutaneous nerve

The human nervous sytem

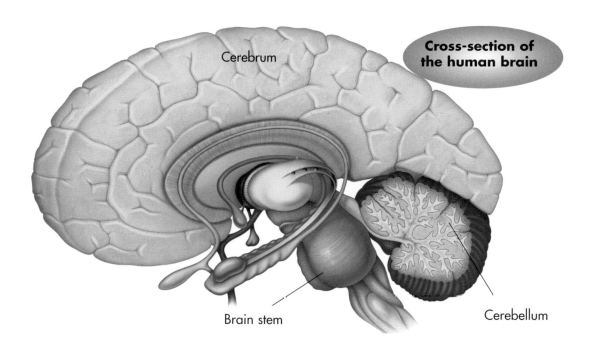

Cerebrum

Cross-section of the human brain

Brain stem

Cerebellum

HOW DOES THE BRAIN WORK?

The brain is the body's control center. It coordinates all the messages that pass through the nervous system, giving us the ability to learn, reason, and feel. It also controls the body's automatic functions, such as breathing, heartbeat, digestion, growth, and blood pressure.

The brain is divided into three main regions, each with a different function. The large part at the top is the cerebrum, where most of our thinking, reasoning, and memory is controlled. The cerebellum is a smaller area at the back, where both accurate movement and coordination are controlled. The brain stem is a small region at the base where most of our automatic body functions are processed and controlled.

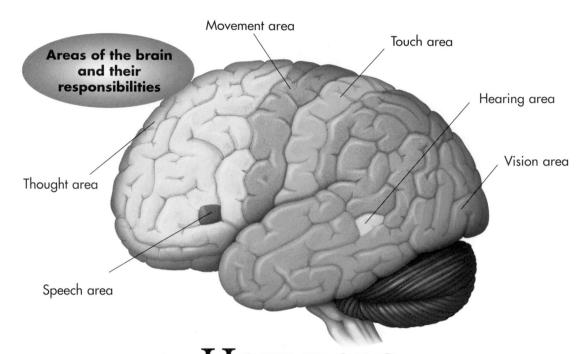

Areas of the brain and their responsibilities

Movement area

Touch area

Hearing area

Vision area

Thought area

Speech area

HOW DOES MEMORY WORK?

Memory is the ability to store things that you experience and learn, ready for use in the future. Some things are remembered easily, such as dramatic events in our life. However, more ordinary things need to be rehearsed several times before they "stick."

There are three different ways of storing memory. Sensory memory, which is very brief, tells what is happening around you and allows you to move without bumping into things. Short-term memory, which lasts about only 30 seconds, allows you to remember a phone number and dial it, but after a minute or so it will vanish. Finally, long-term memory describes things that you have carefully memorized and learned.

FACT FILE

The sense of smell has powerful effects in retrieving memories. Often a smell, like the burning of a bonfire, can suddenly trigger a memory from many years ago.

WHEN DO WE SUFFER FROM REFERRED PAIN?

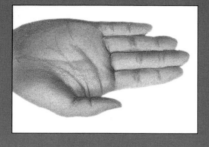

FACT FILE

Some areas of the skin are densely packed with nerve endings, such as the fingertips, while others, as on the back, have comparatively few.

Referred pain is a pain that has a source in one place of the body, but we feel it in another part of the body. Internal organs and structure are well supplied with nerves, but pain is widely spread and poorly located compared with skin sensations. Most pain is caused by stretching and contracting, such as colic. Internal pain will cause stimulation of local nerves in a portion of the spinal cord which makes it appear that the pain is coming from the skin because it is supplied by the sensory nerves.

The heart (**1**) and the esophagus (**2**) refer pain to the neck, shoulders, and arms. The uterus (**3**) and pancreas (**4**) refer pain to the lumbar region. The kidneys (**5**) refer pain into the groin.

Pain from the diaphragm may be referred to the shoulders because the phrenic nerve is formed from the spinal nerves in the neck, which also supply the shoulders.

Referred pain

From the heart

From the esophagus

Pancreas and stomach

Kidney

Gynecological

WHAT ARE THE AREAS OF THE BRAIN CALLED?

The brain can be divided into three different regions: the hindbrain, midbrain, and forebrain. Each of these regions is, in turn, divided into separate areas responsible for quite distinct functions, all intricately linked to other parts of the brain.

The largest structure in the hindbrain is called the *cerebellum*. The largest part of the entire brain is the *cerebrum*, which is located in the forebrain. It is more developed in human beings than in any other animal. This is where the other parts of the brain send incoming messages for decision. The *cerebral cortex* is the thick, wrinkled layer of gray matter folded over the outside of the cerebrum. This part of the brain has become so highly developed in human beings that it has had to fold over and over in order to fit inside the skull. Unfolded, it would cover an area 30 times as large as when folded.

FACT FILE

Shivering is governed by four mechanisms. The hypothalamus, located at the base of the brain, senses that the temperature is too low and sends messages to the thyroid gland, telling it to speed up the metabolic rate. The body muscles then alternately contract and relax rapidly, thus producing heat. The nerves then send messages to the skin and the skin pores narrow, ensuring that heat is conserved within the body.

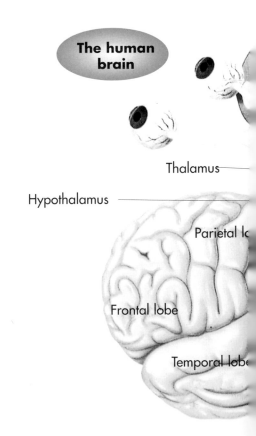

The human brain

Thalamus

Hypothalamus

Parietal l

Frontal lobe

Temporal lob

WHAT ARE THE THREE MAIN FUNCTIONS OF THE BRAIN?

The brain is the body's control center. It keeps the body working smoothly, and it looks after thoughts, feelings, and memory.

Different parts of the brain have different jobs to do. The largest part is called the cerebrum, or forebrain. It looks like a huge half-walnut. The cerebrum's main job is to sort out and respond to messages sent to it from the senses. It also stores information as memory, and it thinks. Messages from the senses are managed by the cerebrum's sensory area, while the motor area controls the muscles.

Thinking, memory, and speech are managed by the parts known as the *association areas*. The cerebellum (or hindbrain) is below the cerebrum. It works with the cerebrum's motor area to ensure that the muscles function smoothly.

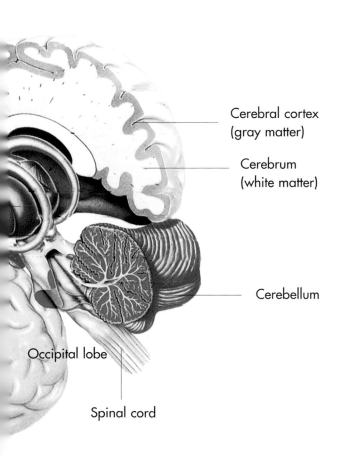

Cerebral cortex
(gray matter)

Cerebrum
(white matter)

Cerebellum

Occipital lobe

Spinal cord

FACT FILE

Although we have invented computers that can work out millions of different things in seconds, our brains can still outwork and outsmart them! Our brains control our bodies by sending out billions of tiny electrical signals every second.

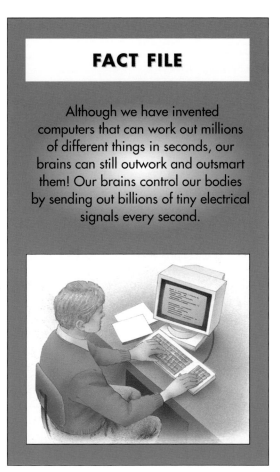

125

WHAT CONTROLS OUR BALANCE?

The inner ear is the body's main organ of balance, but the brain also receives messages from nerve-endings in the neck, back, leg, and foot muscles. The brain sifts all this information and sends messages back to the muscles, allowing us to perform balancing activities, such as ice-skating or gymnastics. Near the cochlea are fluid-filled tubes, called the *semicircular canals*. As your head moves about, the fluid inside each canal swishes to and fro. When the body moves, the fluid causes hairs in a jelly-like mass to bend. These are connected to the vestibular nerve, which alerts the brain to rebalance the body.

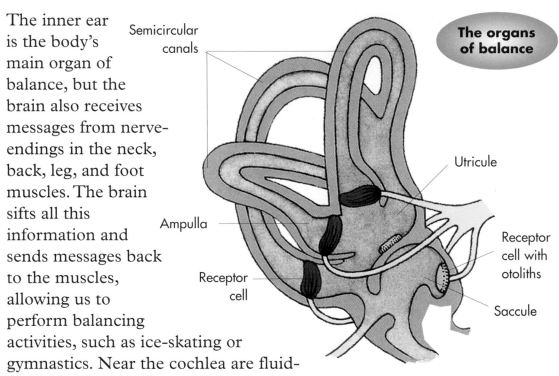

Semicircular canals

The organs of balance

Utricule

Ampulla

Receptor cell

Receptor cell with otoliths

Saccule

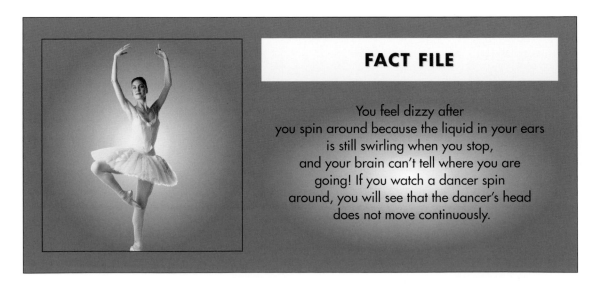

FACT FILE

You feel dizzy after you spin around because the liquid in your ears is still swirling when you stop, and your brain can't tell where you are going! If you watch a dancer spin around, you will see that the dancer's head does not move continuously.

WHAT CONTROLS OUR TEMPERATURE?

FACT FILE

Body movements can also be homeostatic. A hot person may spread out the arms and legs to increase heat loss; a cold person curls up to reduce the areas of the body losing warmth.

Homeostasis means constancy of the internal environment. The body must regulate many body systems and processes to keep inner conditions stable. The temperature nucleus in the hypothalamus controls heat loss and production by the body through the skin. Overheating (**A**) causes an increased blood flow from the blood vessels (**1**) to radiate heat, and causes sweating through the sweat glands (**2**) to lose heat. A fall in body temperature (**B**) constricts the surface blood vessels, stops sweating, and makes the erector muscles (**3**) contract, causing the hairs (**4**) to stand on end, trapping air as an insulating layer. Additional heat can be produced by shivering.

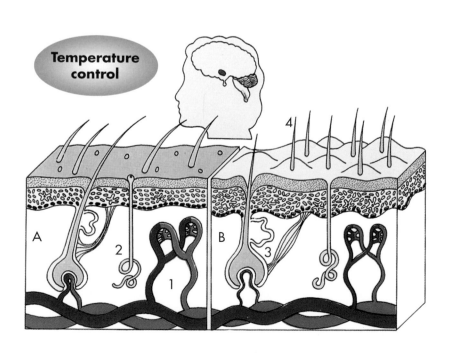

Temperature control

WHEN DOES OUR SENSE OF TOUCH ALERT THE BRAIN OF DANGER?

Close your eyes and touch something, such as your clothes, a table, a car, or even your own skin. Stroke it gently. What does it feel like? Is it hard or soft, hot or cold? The surface may be smooth, bumpy, gritty, furry, or hairy. It could be dry, moist, or slimy. Your skin continually passes large amounts of information to the brain. It monitors touch, pain, temperature, and other factors that tell the brain exactly how the body is being affected by its environment. Without this constant flow of information, you would continually injure yourself accidentally, which happens in rare diseases where skin senses are lost. Senses in the skin are measured by tiny receptors at the ends of nerves. There are several different types of receptors. Each type can detect only one kind of sensation, such as pain, temperature, pressure, and touch.

FACT FILE

Sometimes we need drugs, or analgesics, to control pain. Some drugs, such as aspirin, work by preventing the sensation of pain from reaching the brain.

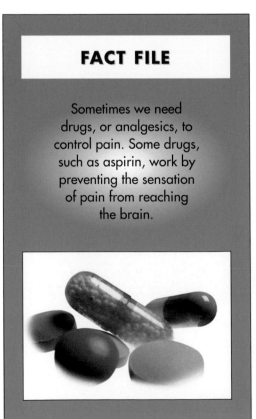

Skin sensation

Hair follicle nerve endings

WHEN DO WE USE OUR BRAIN TO SMELL?

The part of the brain that analyzes messages coming from receiver cells in the nose is closely connected with the limbic system. This is the part of the brain that deals with emotions, moods, and memory. It is called the primitive brain, sometimes even the "smelling brain." This connection explains why smells are closely associated with emotional significance.

Certain smells bring back memories of long-forgotten special occasions, as we tend to remember those things which have special emotional significance. This is because the areas of the brain that process memories are also closely linked to the limbic system, which in turn is linked to the areas in the brain that control the sense of smell.

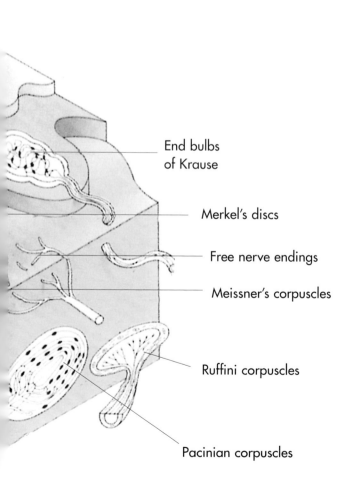

End bulbs of Krause

Merkel's discs

Free nerve endings

Meissner's corpuscles

Ruffini corpuscles

Pacinian corpuscles

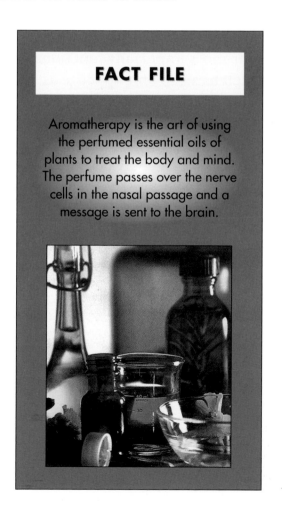

FACT FILE

Aromatherapy is the art of using the perfumed essential oils of plants to treat the body and mind. The perfume passes over the nerve cells in the nasal passage and a message is sent to the brain.

WHERE IS SEROTONIN PRODUCED?

Serotonin is made by cells in the base of the brain from an amino acid called *L-tryptophan*, and is also produced by some skin and blood cells, and in the digestive system. There are more than a dozen kinds of serotonin receptors located in different parts of the body.

Serotonin is actually a chemical that behaves in the brain and other parts of the body to influence various feelings, actions, and processes. It regulates many of our most important functions, such as sleep and appetite as well as aggression and moods. Serotonin is what is known as a *neurotransmitter*, a chemical that carries signals between nerve cells. A powerful agent, serotonin even modifies the effects of other neurotransmitters, and helps shape early brain development. Serotonin is found extensively in other animals and plants in addition to human beings.

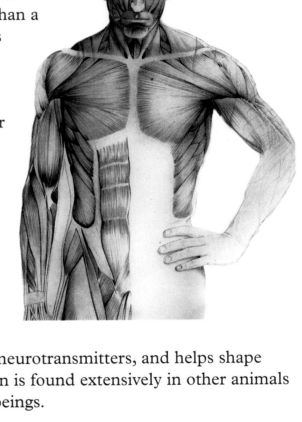

FACT FILE

Because serotonin has an impact in so many ways, many drugs are prescribed to raise serotonin levels in the nervous system, to treat depression, migraine headaches, and schizophrenia.

WHERE IS THE CEREBRUM?

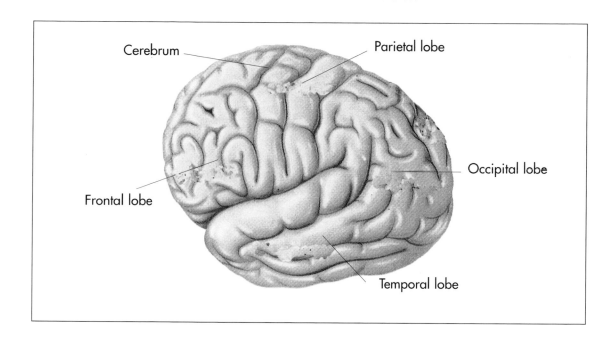

Cerebrum

Parietal lobe

Frontal lobe

Occipital lobe

Temporal lobe

FACT FILE

The brain stem is the vital control area of the brain. It maintains all the essential regulatory mechanisms of the body: respiration, blood pressure, pulse rate, alertness, and sleep.

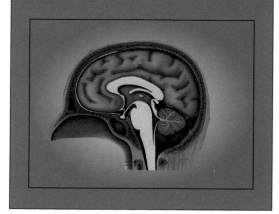

The cerebrum is part of the brain, representing about 85 percent of its weight. It is divided into two halves, the left cerebral hemisphere and the right cerebral hemisphere, by a deep groove called the *longitudinal fissure*.

The hemispheres themselves are joined by bundles of nerves, the largest of which is the *corpus callosum*. These nerves are in turn divided into four lobes. The frontal lobe is at the front, the temporal lobe at the lower side, the parietal lobe in the middle, and the occipital lobe is at the back. Each of these names are the same as the bone of the skull that it lies beneath.

WHY DO WE DREAM?

Whatever we dream, it is touched by our feelings, wishes, memories, fears, and emotions. Other influences can come into play as well. If something is affecting us physically, like cold or hunger, it can often be a part of our dreams. We have all heard of someone who has fallen out of bed and dreamt he or she was falling off a cliff just as the person was about to awake. Psychoanalysts study the reasons for our dreaming, saying that dreams reflect wishes that didn't come true, that a dream is a form of wish fulfillment. According to this line of thinking, when we are asleep our inhibitions are asleep as well.

FACT FILE

Daydreaming is a form of dreaming, done while we are awake. Night dreaming is done while we are asleep. That is the only difference between them, since both are done when the dreamer is so relaxed that he or she pays no attention to what is going on.

WHY DO WE AWAKEN FROM SLEEP?

The short answer is, we don't really know. There are some things about sleep that even scientists find hard to explain. Sometimes we "drop off" to sleep in an instant. Other times we cannot get to sleep no matter how hard we try.

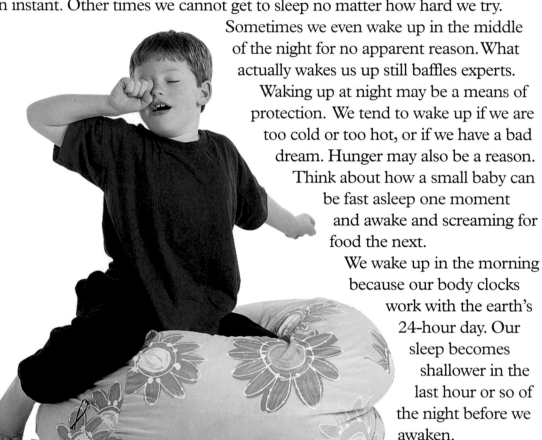

Sometimes we even wake up in the middle of the night for no apparent reason. What actually wakes us up still baffles experts. Waking up at night may be a means of protection. We tend to wake up if we are too cold or too hot, or if we have a bad dream. Hunger may also be a reason. Think about how a small baby can be fast asleep one moment and awake and screaming for food the next.

We wake up in the morning because our body clocks work with the earth's 24-hour day. Our sleep becomes shallower in the last hour or so of the night before we awaken.

FACT FILE

Even while the body sleeps, its nerve systems are active, continuously monitoring and adjusting the internal processes, and checking the outside world for danger. The heart never stops, but beats slower while at rest.

WHY DO WE GET THIRSTY?

All of us have had the experience of being thirsty, but can you imagine how it would feel to be thirsty for days? If a human being has absolutely nothing to drink for a long period, he or she will die. Thirst is simply our body's way of telling us to replenish its liquid supply.

The reason for this thirst is caused by a change in the salt content of our blood. There is a certain normal amount of salt and water in our blood. When this changes and there is more salt in relation to water in our blood, thirst results.

Part of our brain is called the "thirst center." It responds to the amount of salt in our blood. When there is a change, it sends messages to the back of the throat. From there, messages go to the brain, and it is this combination of feelings that makes us say we are thirsty.

FACT FILE

Onions send out an irritating substance when we peel them. The onion has an oil that contains sulphur. This not only gives it its sharp odor, but it also irritates the eye. The eye reacts by blinking and producing tears to wash it away. That is why we cry when we peel onions.

WHY DO WE GET HUNGRY?

Have you ever wondered how your brain gets the message that makes us feel hungry? Hunger has nothing to do with an empty stomach, as most people believe.

When certain nutritive materials are missing from the blood, hunger sets in. The lack of these materials in the blood vessels causes in a message to be sent to a part of the brain called the *lateral hypothalamus*, or "hunger center." The hunger center is a bit like a brake that works on the stomach and the intestine. If there is enough food for the blood, the hunger center slows up the action of the stomach and intestine. When food is missing from the blood, it stimulates the stomach and intestine into more action. That is why when we are hungry we often hear our stomach rumbling.

When we are hungry, we don't want any particular kind of food, our body just needs nourishment. It depends on the individual how long we can actually live without food. A calm person can live longer than an excitable one because the protein stored in his or her body is used up more slowly.

FACT FILE

Eggs are an extremely good source of protein, which is vital for building up and repairing muscles. Milk and dairy products are another good source of protein.

GENETICS AND

REPRODUCTION

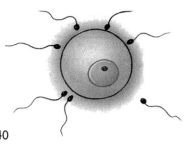

CONTENTS

WHAT HAPPENS TO A BABY IN ITS FIRST YEAR? 140
WHAT ARE CHROMOSOMES? 141

WHAT HAPPENS TO A FERTILIZED EGG? 142
HOW DOES THE BREAST PRODUCE MILK? 143

HOW DOES OUR BODY GROW? 144
HOW DO PEOPLE AGE? 145

WHY SHOULD WE WEAR SUNSCREEN? 146
HOW DO WE GET BROWN EYES? 147

WHEN IS A BABY'S GENETIC MAKEUP DECIDED? 148
WHEN DOES MITOSIS OCCUR? 149

WHEN WERE GENES DISCOVERED? 150
WHEN DO WE LEARN TO TALK? 151

WHY DO SOME PEOPLE WEAR GLASSES? 152
WHEN ARE TWINS CONCEIVED? 153

WHERE IS SPERM PRODUCED? 154
WHY DOES MENSTRUATION TAKE PLACE? 155

WHERE DOES A BABY DEVELOP? 156
WHERE DOES LANUGO FORM ON A FETUS? 157

WHY DO WE HAVE CHROMOSOMES? 158
WHERE DO WE INHERIT OUR TRAITS? 159

WHAT HAPPENS TO A BABY IN ITS FIRST YEAR?

FACT FILE

A baby's personality begins to develop soon after birth. This development continues throughout childhood and life.

The newborn baby lies with his or her knees drawn up. A baby reflexively grasps any object that touches the palm and when held upright, automatically steps as the feet touch something. A baby roots and sucks the nipple automatically. These reflexes disappear within a few weeks. At one month, the baby's legs are straighter and by six weeks, the baby can lift the head. The baby is asleep more than awake, but gradually the eyes move to focus on objects and at about six weeks, smiling begins. By six months, birth weight doubles and the baby can sit unaided. At eight months, gurglings, preliminary speech, are heard and the thumb can be used. At about ten months, crawling begins and birth weight triples. First steps are often taken at a year old. About two or three months later, the first words may be spoken.

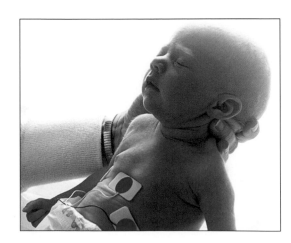

WHAT ARE CHROMOSOMES?

The moment of conception is the most important stage of sexual reproduction. Fertilization is complete when the chromosomes of the male sperm unite with the chromosomes of the female egg. Chromosomes are thread-like structures that contain genes, the units of heredity that determine each person's unique traits. Most body cells have 46 chromosomes that occur in 23 pairs. However, as each egg or sperm develops, it undergoes a special series of cell divisions called *meiosis*. As a result, each sperm or egg cell

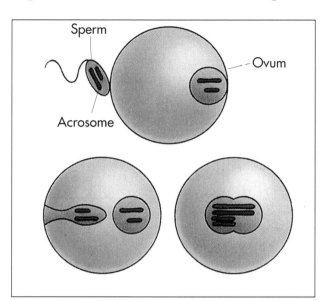

contains only one member of each chromosome pair, or 23 unpaired chromosomes. During fertilization, the chromosomes pair up so that the fertilized egg has the normal number of 46 chromosomes. Only about 100 sperm survive the journey of nearly 24 hours, and only one fertilizes the ovum. The sperm's acrosome disappears as it dissolves the membrane of the ovum. The tail and body are shed when the head penetrates to join its 23 chromosomes with those of the ovarian nucleus.

FACT FILE

Special sex chromosomes determine whether the zygote will develop into a boy or a girl. Each body cell contains a pair of sex chromosomes. In females, the two sex chromosomes are identical.

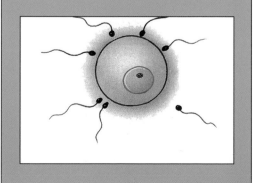

WHAT HAPPENS TO A FERTILIZED EGG?

A fertilized egg (or zygote) goes through a series of changes before it reaches the uterus. In the uterus, the zygote develops into a form called

Morula

the *embryo*, which develops rapidly. The zygote then travels through the fallopian tube toward the uterus. Along the way, the zygote begins to divide rapidly into many cells with no increase in overall size. The resulting cell mass is called a *morula*. By the third or fourth day, the morula enters the uterus and the embryo develops from the central cells of the morula. They develop into the *placenta*, a special organ that enables the embryo to obtain food and oxygen from the mother. After the morula enters the uterus, it continues to divide. At this stage, the ball of cells is called a *blastocyst*. The cells of the blastocyst divide as it floats in the

Blastocyst

uterus for one or two days. About the fifth or sixth day of pregnancy, the blastocyst becomes attached to the internal surface of the uterus. The

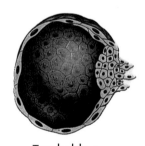

Trophoblast

outer cells of the blastocyst, called the *trophoblast*, secrete an enzyme that breaks down the lining of the uterus. The trophoblast begins to divide rapidly, invading the uterine tissue. The process of attachment to the uterine wall is called *implantation*.

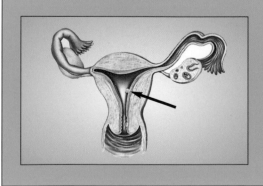

FACT FILE

By the 11th day of pregnancy, the blastocyst is firmly implanted in the uterus. Various structures develop in the uterus to help the embryo grow. These structures include the placenta and certain membranes.

HOW DOES THE BREAST PRODUCE MILK?

Two pituitary hormones are responsible for the production of breast milk. Prolactin stimulates the breast to produce milk, and oxytocin starts milk flow. The baby's sucking of the nipples also stimulates lactation. A mother's milk is a complete source of food and energy for the baby. It also contains antibodies which protect the infant from many diseases. The breast is an organ specially designed to produce milk

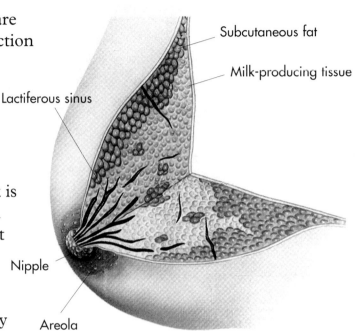

Subcutaneous fat

Milk-producing tissue

Lactiferous sinus

Nipple

Areola

to feed the baby. All human beings have two breasts, but only mature females can produce milk.

The breast is composed of 15 to 20 modified sweat glands that develop into lobes. The female breast gland develops rapidly at puberty and secretes cells responding to the hormones in the menstrual cycle.

During pregnancy, the glands become congested, and milk is collected in the lactiferous sinuses, which are joined behind the areola of the nipple. The areola is lubricated by the moist secretion of sebaceous glands.

FACT FILE

Breast milk is secreted by the lining of the alveoli (below). As the baby feeds, the milk is drawn down the ducts, from where it is sucked out of the nipple.

HOW DOES OUR BODY GROW?

The human body has the following stages of growth: embryo and fetus, infant, child, youth, mature adult, and old age. People's bodies grow faster in the first weeks of life than at any other time. Even before the end of the first year, bodies are growing less rapidly. Through the whole period of childhood, bodies grow at a moderate rate. Then the growth starts to speed up again. All human beings are much alike in their growth, but there are important differences. Boys and girls follow the same general pathway of growth, but each follows it in his or her own way.

Growth stages of a human fetus before birth

4 weeks

8 weeks

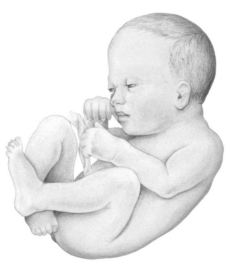

12 weeks

40 weeks

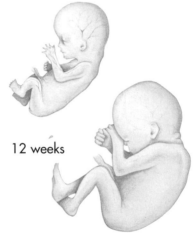

20 weeks

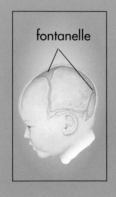

fontanelle

FACT FILE

The bones of a baby's head are not fused at birth, making the skull flexible enough to pass through the mother's birth canal. The bones eventually join, but a gap in the skull, called the *fontanelle*, may not close up for several months.

30 weeks

144

HOW DO PEOPLE AGE?

Aging results from the gradual failure of the body's cells and organs to replace and repair themselves. There is a limit to the number of times that each cell can divide. As the body's cells begin to near this limit, the rate at which they divide begins to slow down. Sometimes the new cells that are produced have defects or do not carry out their usual task effectively. Organs can then begin to fail, tissues will change in structure, and the chemical reactions that power the body become less efficient. Sometimes the blood supply to the brain is not effective. The brain cells become starved of oxygen and nutrients, leading to forgetfulness. For most elderly people, memories bring great pleasure. Strangely, even though recent events may be forgotten, elderly people often clearly remember events that took place in their childhood.

FACT FILE

The skin becomes looser as people age. As skin sags, it forms wrinkles and creases because the fibers of collagen that normally provide support to the skin become weaker.

WHY SHOULD WE WEAR SUNSCREEN?

FACT FILE

Skin develops extra melanin when it is exposed to strong sunlight. Tiny grains are produced in the skin cells and spread to produce an even suntan which helps protect against sun damage. You can get sunburned if you expose yourself too long to the sun. You should always wear protective sun cream and cover your head.

Almost everyone's skin cells contain tiny granules of a chemical called *melanin*. The amount varies during the year, according to how much sun an individual has been exposed to. The function of melanin is to protect the skin from being damaged by ultraviolet rays from the sun, which can cause skin cancer. This is particularly important in places like Australia, South Africa, and South America, as well as northern Europe and North America, where the ozone layer in the atmosphere is thinning. The result of this thinning means that more ultraviolet rays are reaching the surface of the earth. This is why skin cancer rates are higher than they have ever been.

Wearing sunscreen helps reduce our exposure to ultraviolet rays, consequently lowering our risk of skin cancer.

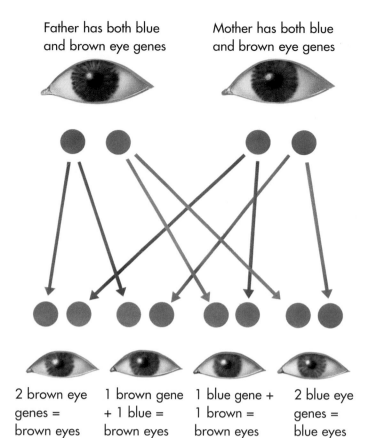

Father has both blue and brown eye genes

Mother has both blue and brown eye genes

2 brown eye genes = brown eyes

1 brown gene + 1 blue = brown eyes

1 blue gene + 1 brown = brown eyes

2 blue eye genes = blue eyes

HOW DO WE GET BROWN EYES?

FACT FILE

This DNA molecule is shaped like a ladder twisted into a spiral. The pattern in which these are formed is the code built into the DNA molecule and groups of these form genes.

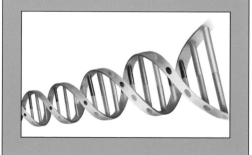

Although genes from both parents are mixed together at fertilization, some genes have a stronger effect than others. These *dominant* genes override the effects of others, which are called *recessive* genes. For example, if a child has a gene for brown eyes from one parent, and a gene for blue eyes from the other, the child will always have brown eyes. This is because the gene for brown eyes is the dominant gene.

However, two parents with brown eyes may have children with blue eyes if the parents carry the blue eyes gene. This means that a child would get the recessive blue gene from both parents.

WHEN IS A BABY'S GENETIC MAKEUP DECIDED?

A baby's genetic make-up is decided when the egg is fertilized and a set of chromosomes from the mother combines with a different set of chromosomes from the father. Each nucleus contains two sets of genes. One came originally from the baby's father and one from the mother. Before a cell divides, both sets of genes are copied. This is called *DNA replication*. Each new offspring cell then receives a full double set of genes, one from the father and one from the mother. Every cell in the baby's body, except its own sperm or eggs, which will have only one set of chromosomes, will have the same genetic make-up as this first cell.

Because each human body receives half its genes from each parent, it inherits some of the features of each parent. This is why all kinds of characteristics, such as height, run in families.

The most obvious characteristic inherited from a father is whether a baby is a boy or a girl. This is determined by whether the sperm contains an X chromosome (girl) or a Y chromosome (boy). Other characteristics are determined by whether both parents carry the same gene, for instance for brown eyes or black hair, or whether one parent carries a dominant gene, which always overrules the recessive gene.

Mitosis – cell reproduction

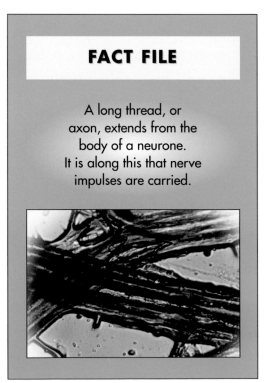

FACT FILE

A long thread, or axon, extends from the body of a neurone. It is along this that nerve impulses are carried.

WHEN DOES MITOSIS OCCUR?

The DNA of chromosomes has the ability to reproduce itself. Without this, cells could not pass on information from one generation to the next. The process of cell division by which the cell duplicates itself is called *mitosis*. This works in the following manner:

1. The chromosomes become shorter and the nuclear envelope breaks.
2. The chromosomes are released and duplicate and attach themselves to a cytoplasmic network.
3. Then are drawn apart.
4–7. They form two new cells with reformed nuclear envelopes.

Mitosis is absolutely essential to life because it provides new cells for growth and for replacement of worn-out cells. Mitosis may take minutes or hours, depending upon the kind of cells and species of organisms. It is influenced by time of day, temperature, and chemicals. Strictly speaking, the term *mitosis* is used to describe the duplication and distribution of chromosomes, the structures that carry our genetic information.

FACT FILE

DNA strands look like a twisted ladder. Sections of DNA are called *genes*. All the instructions for growing a new human being are coded into the DNA molecule.

WHEN WERE GENES DISCOVERED?

In the 1800s, a monk named Gregor Mendel experimented with characteristics in pea plants by cross-fertilizing plants with different traits. He kept careful track of the traits displayed by the pea plants produced by cross-fertilization, discovering that the characteristics from the parent plants were inherited by the progeny plants in specific patterns.

Mendel also discovered during his experiments that some genes were more dominant than others. For example, if a pea with a white flower is cross-fertilized with a pea with a pink flower, the resulting flowers will all be pink.

This is seen in human beings. For example, if a child has a gene for brown eyes from one parent and a gene for blue eyes from the other, the child will always have brown eyes. This is because the gene for brown eyes is a dominant gene.

Model of DNA

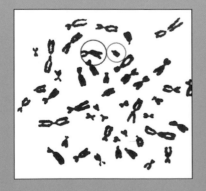

FACT FILE

Chromosomes are tiny threads that are present in all cells apart from red blood cells. They contain all the information needed for an entire person to develop. There are 46 chromosomes in each cell. They come in 22 pairs, plus another special pair that determine the person's sex.

WHEN DO WE LEARN TO TALK?

As air flows out of the lungs, we can use it to make the sounds of speech and other noises. At the top of the windpipe, at the sides of the voice box, or larynx, are two stiff, shelf-like folds called the vocal cords. Criss-crossed muscles in the voice box pull the vocal cords together so that air passes through a narrow slit between them, making them vibrate, which creates sounds. As the vocal cords are pulled tighter, they make higher-pitched sounds. As the vocal cords loosen, they make lower-pitched sounds. When we learn to talk depends on the development of the brain and its ability to copy the sounds that we hear.

FACT FILE

Although many people think of speech as our main way of communicating, we do not have to use spoken words. People who cannot speak learn a language called *signing*, in which hands and fingers are used to signal letters and words.

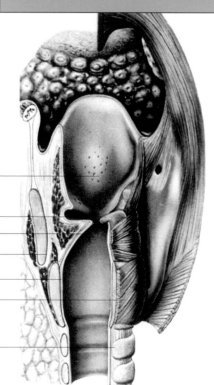

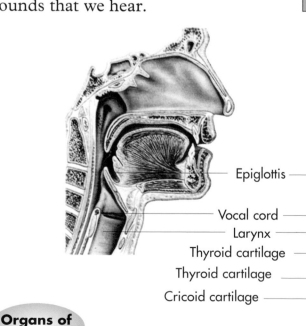

Epiglottis

Vocal cord

Larynx

Thyroid cartilage

Thyroid cartilage

Cricoid cartilage

Organs of speech

Trachea: *C*-shaped cartilages

WHY DO SOME PEOPLE WEAR EYEGLASSES?

If the eye is not correctly shaped or if the lens cannot focus properly, you cannot form a clear image on the retina. In this case, you may need to wear eyeglasses to correct your vision. For a person who is near-sighted, distant objects look blurred. This is because the image forms in front of the retina. A near-sighted person can see nearby objects very clearly. For a person who is far-sighted, the images try to form behind the retina. Nearby images are blurred because the lens tries to focus on a nearby object. Both conditions can be inherited from parents. As people get older, the lenses of their eyes grow harder and cannot change their shape to focus close up.

FACT FILE

Blinking is a very important function. It cleans and lubricates the surface of the eye. In particular, the cornea is a sensitive area and must be protected from drying out and infection.

lens

retina

cornea iris

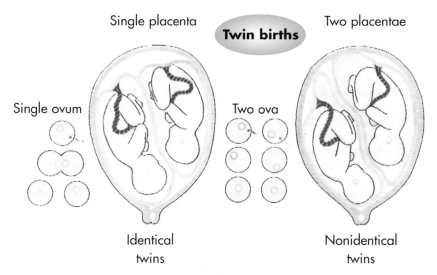

Twin births

Single placenta

Two placentae

Single ovum

Two ova

Identical twins

Nonidentical twins

WHEN ARE TWINS CONCEIVED?

A baby begins as a fertilized egg–a pinhead-sized egg cell from the mother, which has joined an even smaller tadpole-shaped sperm cell from the father. Although thousands of these sperm cells may cluster around the egg cell, only one of these will actually fertilize the egg.

Nonidentical twins are produced when two eggs are released at the same time and both are fertilized. They can be the same sex, or brother and sister.

Identical twins are produced when the embryo splits into two in the early stages of its development. This produces two identical children of the same sex. Some identical twins look so much alike that they can be told apart only by their fingerprints. Only one in 83 pregnancies results in twins.

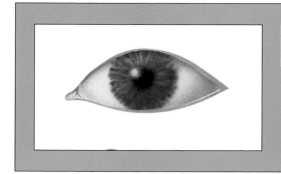

FACT FILE

Identical twins share the same physical traits: identical eye color, hair color, and other characteristics. Nonidentical twins are only as alike as any other pair of siblings.

153

WHERE IS SPERM PRODUCED?

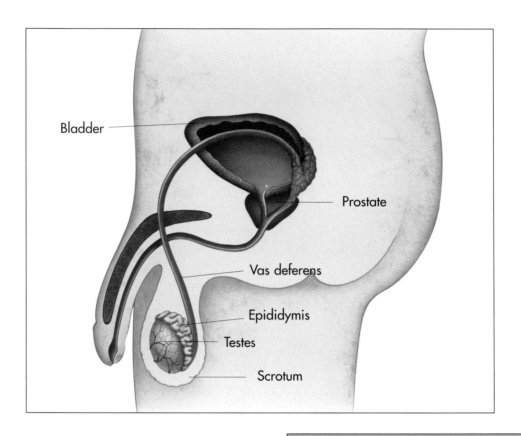

Bladder

Prostate

Vas deferens

Epididymis

Testes

Scrotum

Sperm, the male sex cells, develop in the testes. It is stored for several days until needed. The testes contain long tubes called the *seminiferous tubules*, which are tightly coiled. Sperm is produced continuously in these tubes, then passed to the epididymis and stored in a large duct called the *vas deferens*. Here, liquid is added to the sperm to make a milky fluid called *semen*. It is stored in pouches called *seminal vesicles*. During sexual intercourse, the seminal vesicles contract and force out the sperm.

FACT FILE

Up to 100 million sperms are produced every day by the male. If they are not released, they are soon destroyed and replaced. Sperms look like tiny tadpoles with rounded heads and long, lashing tails.

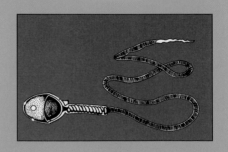

WHY DOES MENSTRUATION TAKE PLACE?

FACT FILE

The ovary is one of a pair of female sex organs that store and release eggs. The human ovary is oval in shape and about the size of an unshelled walnut.

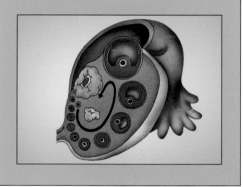

Most women of child-bearing age experience menstruation, the loss of blood and cells through the vagina that takes place on a monthly basis. The uterus, or womb, is the oval-shaped organ that holds a baby during pregnancy, and each month blood and cells build up in its lining. This lining thickens in preparation for pregnancy. If pregnancy does not occur, the lining breaks down. The blood and cells are then discharged through a canal that leads from the uterus to the outside of the body. This canal is the vagina. The menstruation process can last from three to seven days. This time is known as the menstrual period.

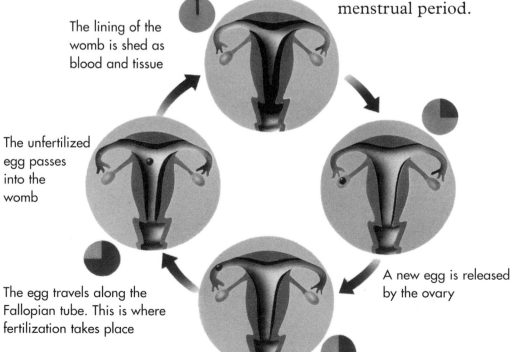

The lining of the womb is shed as blood and tissue

The unfertilized egg passes into the womb

The egg travels along the Fallopian tube. This is where fertilization takes place

A new egg is released by the ovary

WHERE DOES A BABY DEVELOP?

A baby develops in the uterus, or womb–a hollow, muscular organ in the mother's abdomen. The period of development in the uterus lasts about nine months, in most cases. During this time, development is more rapid than at any time after birth.

For a baby to develop, a sperm from the father must unite with an egg from the mother. This union of a sperm and an egg is called *fertilization*. It produces a single cell called a fertilized egg. By a series of remarkable changes, the fertilized egg gradually develops into a baby.

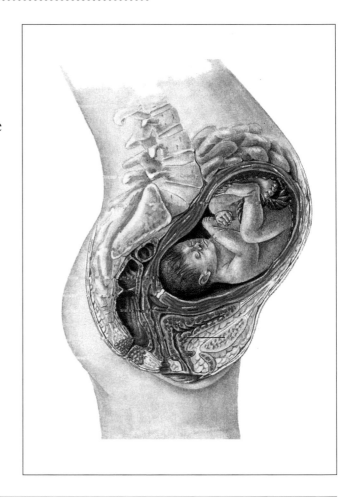

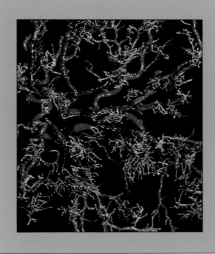

FACT FILE

The placenta is an organ composed largely of blood vessels. The placenta is attached to the wall of the uterus. A tube-like structure called the *umbilical cord* joins the placenta to the embryo at the abdomen. The placenta supplies everything that the embryo needs to live and grow.

WHERE DOES LANUGO FORM ON A FETUS?

By the fifth month of pregnancy, fine hair called *lanugo* covers the body of the fetus. Lanugo disappears late in pregnancy or shortly after birth. Hair also appears on the head.

From the ninth week of pregnancy until birth, the developing baby is called a *fetus*. In the first three months of this period, the fetus increases rapidly in length. It grows about 2 inches (5 cm) in each of these months. In the later stages of pregnancy, the most striking change in the fetus is in its weight. Most fetuses gain about 25 ounces (700 grams) in both the eighth and ninth months of pregnancy. The mother can feel the movements of the fetus by the fifth month of pregnancy. The eyelids open by the 26th week of pregnancy. By the 28th week, the fingernails and toenails are well developed. Until the 30th week of pregnancy, the fetus appears reddish and transparent because the skin is thin and there is a lack of fat beneath the skin. In the last six to eight weeks before birth, fat develops rapidly, and the fetus becomes smooth and plump.

FACT FILE

In most cases, a single egg is fertilized and develops into one baby. Occasionally, however, two or more infants develop and are born at the same time. The birth of more than one baby from the same pregnancy is called *multiple birth*.

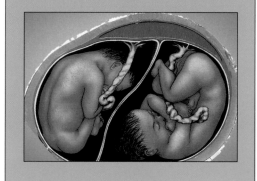

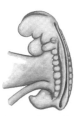 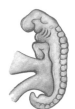 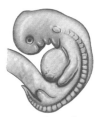

3-week embryo   4-week embryo   5-week embryo

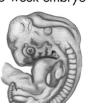  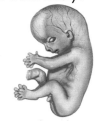

6-week embryo   7-week embryo   8-week embryo

WHY DO WE HAVE CHROMOSOMES?

Every cell has a nucleus which is full of information coded in the form of a chemical called *deoxyribonucleic acid* (or DNA). DNA is organized into groups called *genes*. Every chromosome contains thousands of genes, each with enough information for the production of one protein. This protein may have a small effect within the cell and on the appearance of the body. It may make all the difference between a person having brown or blue eyes, or straight or curly hair.

At the moment the mother's egg is fertilized, the genes start issuing instructions for molding a new human being. Every characteristic that we inherit from our parents is passed on to us through the coding of the genes within the chromosomes.

In rare cases, some people have 47 chromosomes. This occurs when people inherit Downs Syndrome, a genetic disorder.

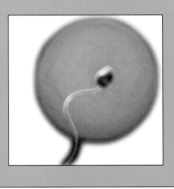

FACT FILE

A baby begins to form when two special cells meet—a sperm cell from a man's body and an egg cell from a woman's body. Joined inside the woman's body, these two cells grow into a whole new person.

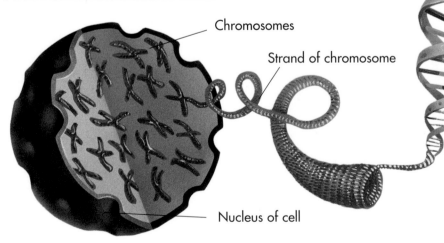

Chromosomes

Strand of chromosome

Rings of pairs of amino acids

DNA strand looks like a twisted ladder

Nucleus of cell

WHERE DO WE INHERIT OUR TRAITS?

Living things inherit characteristics, often called *traits*, from their parents through heredity. Heredity is the passing on of biological characteristics from one generation to the next. The process of heredity occurs among all living things – animals, plants, and even such microscopic organisms as bacteria. Heredity explains why a human mother always has a human baby and why a mother dog has puppies and not kittens. It is also the reason offspring look like their parents. You resemble your parents because you inherited your hair, nose shape, and other traits from them. All organisms consist of cells. Tiny biochemical structures inside each cell, called *genes*, carry traits from one generation to the next.

FACT FILE

You may look like your parents, but you are not an exact duplicate of either of them. You inherited half your genes from your father and half from your mother.

GENERAL KNOWLEDGE

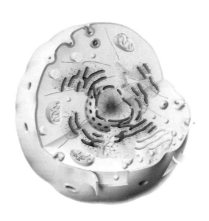

CONTENTS

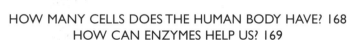

WHEN DO WE LOSE OUR BABY TEETH? 162
WHAT'S INSIDE A TOOTH? 163

HOW DOES OUR IMMUNE SYSTEM WORK? 164
HOW DO FINGERPRINTS DIFFER? 165

WHAT MAKES HAIR CURLY? 166
WHERE ARE FOLLICLES FOUND? 167

HOW MANY CELLS DOES THE HUMAN BODY HAVE? 168
HOW CAN ENZYMES HELP US? 169

HOW FAST DOES HAIR GROW? 170
HOW DO TEETH DIFFER? 171

WHAT IS A TRANSPLANT? 172
WHAT IS INSIDE AN ANIMAL CELL? 173

WHEN DO CELLS DIE? 174
WHEN DOES THE BODY REPLACE DAMAGED CELLS? 175

WHERE ARE OUR ADENOIDS? 176
WHERE ARE OUR VOCAL CORDS? 177

WHY IS WATER GOOD FOR US? 178
WHY ARE CELLS IMPORTANT? 179

WHY DO PEOPLE GET ALLERGIES? 180
WHY DO SOME PEOPLE GET ASTHMA? 181

WHY DO WE STOP GROWING? 182
WHY DON'T WOMEN HAVE BEARDS? 183

WHY DOES OUR TEMPERATURE RISE WHEN WE'RE ILL? 184
WHY IS THE BODY WARM? 185

WHY DO WE TAKE ANTIBIOTICS? 186
HOW ARE VIRUSES DIFFERENT FROM BACTERIA? 187

WHAT IS IMMUNITY? 188
WHY CAN'T WE CURE THE COMMON COLD? 189

WHAT MAKES PEOPLE LAUGH? 190
WHERE WAS THE FIRST ANESTHETIC USED? 191

WHAT WAS THE FIRST PAINKILLER USED? 192
HOW MUCH ENERGY DO WE NEED? 193

WHAT IS MRI? 194
WHY DO WE PERSPIRE? 195

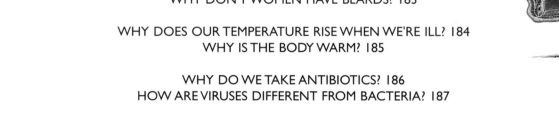

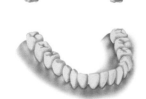

WHEN DO WE LOSE OUR BABY TEETH?

The first set of teeth we have is the baby, milk, or deciduous teeth. Even before birth, teeth appear as tiny buds below the gums. They begin to show above the gum at approximately six months. By around age three, all 20 first teeth have usually appeared. At around age six, the first teeth fall out. These are replaced by the adult, second, or permanent teeth. The front incisors usually appear first, followed by the first molars, at around seven to eight years. The last teeth to appear are the rear-most molars, or wisdom teeth. Some adults never grow wisdom teeth. In many cases, the jaws do not grow large enough to provide space for the wisdom teeth. As a result, the wisdom teeth may become impacted–that is, wedged between the jawbone and another tooth. Then, wisdom teeth must be removed.

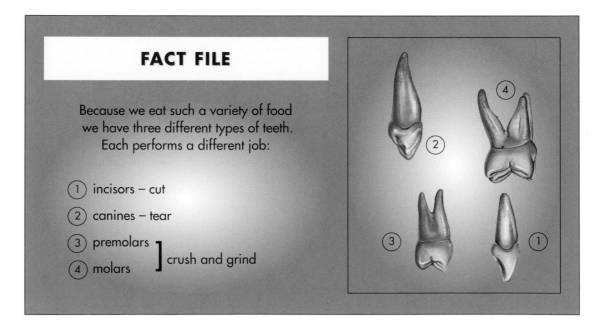

FACT FILE

Because we eat such a variety of food we have three different types of teeth. Each performs a different job:

1. incisors – cut
2. canines – tear
3. premolars ⎤
4. molars   ⎦ crush and grind

WHAT'S INSIDE A TOOTH?

The tooth is made up of four kinds of tissues: pulp, dentine, enamel, and cementum.

Within the pulp, the innermost layer of the tooth, there is connective tissue, blood vessels that nourish the tooth and the nerves which send sensations of pain–including toothache–to the brain.

Surrounding the pulp is a hard yellow substance called *dentine*, which makes up most of a tooth. Harder than bone, dentine consists mostly of water and mineral salts and water but also has some living cells.

In the crown of the tooth the dentine is covered with an outer layer of enamel. Because a tooth has to withstand the pressures involved in chewing, enamel is the hardest tissue in the entire human body. At the root of the tooth, dentine is overlayed with *cementum*. Where the cementum and enamel meet is where the root ends and the crown begins. The tooth grows farther out of its socket, exposing the root, as the outer surface of the tooth deteriorates.

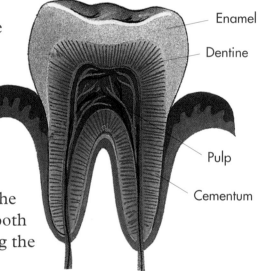

Enamel

Dentine

Pulp

Cementum

FACT FILE

Sometimes teeth grow crookedly or become overcrowded in the mouth. This can be corrected by wearing braces. Braces consist of metal or clear ceramic brackets that are bonded on the front surface of each tooth and connected by wires.

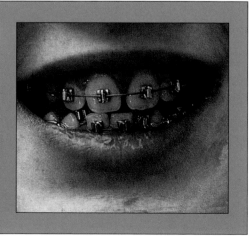

HOW DOES OUR IMMUNE SYSTEM WORK?

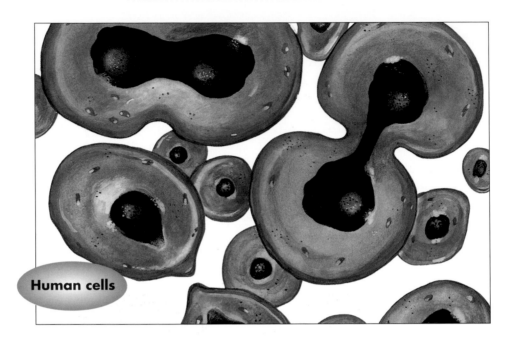

Human cells

The major defense the human body has against diseases and other dangers from outside is with a group of cells, molecules, and tissues we call the *immune system*. It protects the body against a whole range of potentially damaging substances. Our ability to ward off these invaders, such as bacteria, fungi, parasites, and viruses, is called *immunity*.

One of the essential characteristics of the immune system is that it is able to destroy the foreign organisms without affecting the healthy tissues in the body. On the rare occasion when this doesn't happen, the reaction is known as an *autoimmune response*, or *autoimmunity*.

FACT FILE

The immune response is the body's reaction to the invasion of foreign substances by the production of white blood cells known as *lymphocytes*. Lymphocytes are mainly produced in bone marrow.

LYMPHOCYTES

How do Fingerprints Differ?

Fingerprints have fascinated people for centuries. They have been used as a method of personal identification since ancient times. But where do fingerprints come from, and is it true that they are all different? If you look very closely at a fingerprint, you will notice that it is made up of ridges on your skin. These ridges aren't always continuous; they stop,

split into two, form little pockets, called "lakes," and even appear to cross each other at times. It is these individual features that make one fingerprint different from the next.

Fingerprints are formed before birth, during the development of the hands. Fingerprints aren't actually formed in the skin but are caused by ridges in the flesh underneath the skin. Genetics plays some part in their formation, but even identical twins have different fingerprints. Fingerprints fall into a set number of patterns, which allows us to catalog them and perform fingerprint searches more easily.

FACT FILE

How do you leave a fingerprint at a scene of a crime? Skin pores produce oils and sweat, which are distributed on your fingers. When you touch something, those liquids are left on the surface, in the shape of your fingerprints.

WHAT MAKES HAIR CURLY?

Skin feels smooth, but under a microscope it looks like a jagged mountain range with huge pits sprouting hair. These pits are called *follicles*, and they make hair straight or curly. Straight hair grows from a round follicle (1), wavy hair grows from an oval-shaped one (2), and very curly hair grows from a flat one (3).

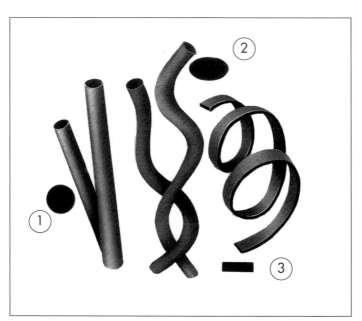

The texture of hair depends mostly on the shape of the hair, which can be seen in cross section under a microscope. Straight hairs have a round shape, and wavy and curly hairs are flat. The flattest hairs are the waviest or curliest. The number of hairs you have on your head depends on whether you are a blonde or brunette. Most blondes have about 140,000 head hairs, red-heads average 90,000, while people with black or brown hair are somewhere in the middle with about 110,000 hairs.

Most hair follicles contain an oil gland called the *sebaceous gland*. This gland secretes oil into the follicle. The oil flows over the hair, lubricating it and keeping it soft.

FACT FILE

Most people's hair gradually becomes gray or white as they grow older, because the pigment called *melanin*, which gives hair its shade, no longer forms.

WHERE ARE FOLLICLES FOUND?

Follicles are found at the root of an individual hair. A follicle is a long tunnel that reaches into the lower layers of the skin. At the end of the tiny tunnel, there is a hair papilla. The papilla is where most of the growth takes place because that is where nutrients are taken up from the blood.

Slightly below the surface of the skin there are sebaceous glands which supply the hair with sufficient sebum, the fatty secretion of these glands. A tiny hair-raising muscle is responsible for providing sebum from the sebaceous glands.

FACT FILE

Fingernails and toenails are made from a different form of the protein that makes up hair, called *keratin*. Keratin is also found in the skin, horses's hooves, and the shells of shrimp.

Cross-section of a nail

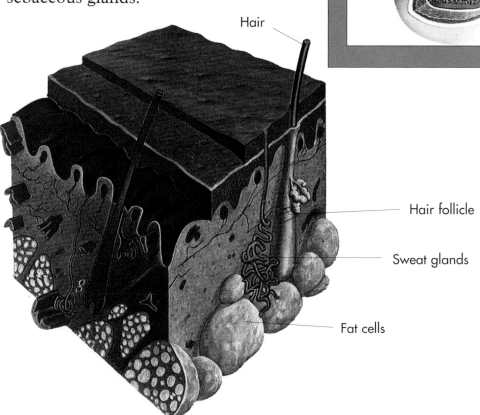

Hair

Hair follicle

Sweat glands

Fat cells

HOW MANY CELLS DOES THE HUMAN BODY HAVE?

FACT FILE

All cells have some things in common, whether they are specialized cells or one-celled organisms. A cell is alive—as alive as you are. It "breathes," takes in food, and gets rid of wastes. It also grows and reproduces and, in time, dies.

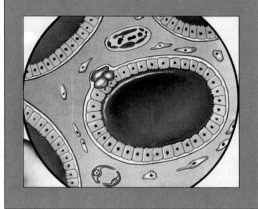

The human body has more than 10 trillion (10,000,000,000,000) cells. A cell is the basic unit of all life and all living things are made up of them.

Most cells are so small they can be seen only with a microscope. It would take about 40,000 red blood cells to fill this letter *O*. It takes millions of cells to make up the skin on the palm of your hand. Some one-celled organisms lead independent lives. Others live in loosely organized groups. As you read these words, for example, nerve cells in your eyes are carrying messages of what you are reading to your brain cells. Muscle cells attached to your eyeballs are moving your eyes across the page.

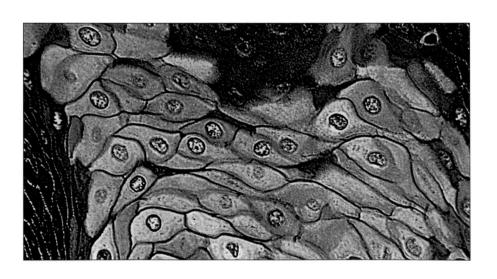

HOW CAN ENZYMES HELP US?

The function of the molecule known as an *enzyme* is to speed up the chemical reaction in living things. Without them, reactions would slow down or simply not happen, and life would be impossible. There are thousands of types of enzymes in the human body. Without them, we could not move, see, digest food, or breathe.

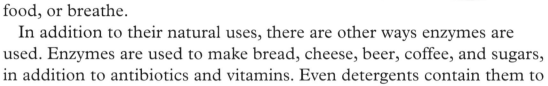

In addition to their natural uses, there are other ways enzymes are used. Enzymes are used to make bread, cheese, beer, coffee, and sugars, in addition to antibiotics and vitamins. Even detergents contain them to break down the protein or fats that cause stains. They are used in medicines to dissolve blood clots, to assist in cleaning wounds, to relieve some types of leukemia, and to check allergic reactions to penicillin. Certain diseases, such as cancer, leukemia, anemia, and heart and liver ailments, can be diagnosed by measuring the level of enzymes in blood and other body fluids.

FACT FILE

The application of enzymes in the future could bring many benefits. They could eliminate spilled oil infecting oceans and lakes, converting it into food for sea plants, and also be used to change raw sewage into useable products.

HOW FAST DOES HAIR GROW?

Although our hair grows at different speeds throughout the day, even at its quickest it's not fast enough for us to see.

These speeds of growth follow a kind of rhythm, with the hair growing slower at night and speeding up with daybreak. It grows at its fastest between 10 and 11 A.M., then slows down again. It speeds up again between 4 and 6 P.M., slowing once more as night approaches.

Of course, all these rates of growth are imperceptibly slow because hair growth is only about half an inch (1.5cm) a month.

FACT FILE

The amount of hair we have varies and is partly determined by actual hair color. A blonde person's hair tends to be finer, but more profuse than that of dark-haired people, while redheads have the least, and coarsest, hair.

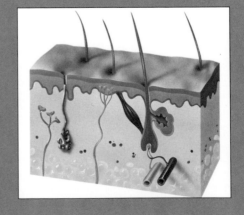

HOW DO TEETH DIFFER?

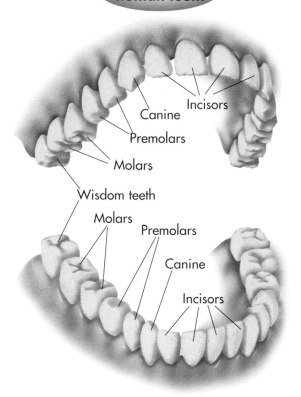

A set of human teeth

Incisors
Canine
Premolars
Molars
Wisdom teeth
Molars
Premolars
Canine
Incisors

Your first set of teeth are called *milk teeth*. These teeth grow beneath the gum and have to force their way out. This process is called *teething*, and can be very painful. Human beings have 20 milk teeth.

Later, another set of teeth form in the gum, under the first set. This second set of teeth gradually pushes the milk teeth out until there are 32 permanent teeth.

Teeth have different shapes so that they can carry out different jobs. Incisor teeth at the front of the mouth are flat and shaped like chisels.

They are used to cut food. The canines are the pointed teeth just behind the incisors, and they are used to tear food.

The back teeth, called molars and premolars, are flattened so they can grind the food into small pieces ready for swallowing. Wisdom teeth, the last teeth in the mouth, are a mystery. No one knows exactly why human beings have them and what their function is.

FACT FILE

Babies are usually born without teeth, as they survive on only milk for the first few months of their lives.

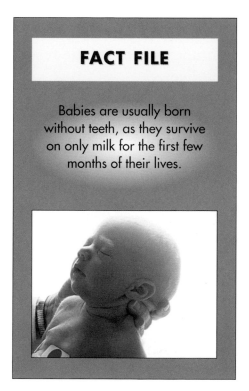

WHAT IS A TRANSPLANT?

In medical terms, a transplant is the removal of an organ from a person, called a *donor*, to give it to another person to prolong or improve his or her quality of life. Different organs of the body can be transplanted, including the heart, kidneys, lungs, corneas, bone marrow, and skin. The donor and the recipient must have closely matching tissue types. This is so that the recipient's immune system is less likely to reject the organ because it sees it as a foreign body. Even so, most organ transplant recipients have to take drugs to suppress their immune system for the rest of their lives.

Many bone marrow donations are taken from the recipient's family members. They provide the best tissue match. Skin transplants are often taken from another part of the recipient's own body.

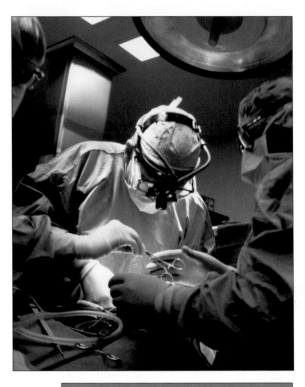

FACT FILE

The first heart transplant was carried out in Cape Town, South Africa, in 1967 by Dr Christian Barnard. The 59-year-old recipient died 18 days later of pneumonia, but patients now survive for many years.

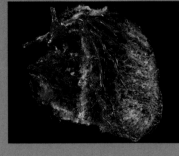

WHAT IS INSIDE AN ANIMAL CELL?

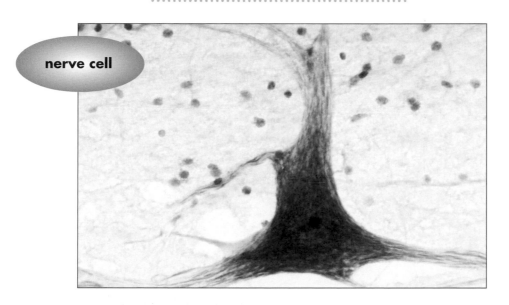

nerve cell

All living things, plant and animal, are made from cells. These cells consist mostly of a watery, jelly-like material called *cytoplasm*. Each cell is held together by a very thin flexible membrane, much like a balloon filled with water. Inside the cell the cytoplasm is organized into special areas called *organelles*. These control the functioning of the cell, for example, the production of essential substances called *proteins*. Tiny organelles called *mitochondria* use oxygen to break down food and release the energy that powers the cell. An area called the *nucleus* contains 46 thread-like chromosomes that control the working of the cell. Some cells, such as those lining the intestines, live for only a few days, while other nerve cells within the brain can survive throughout a lifetime.

FACT FILE

Cells need food, oxygen, and a watery environment in order to survive. Food and water are supplied by the blood and other body fluids, which also carry away wastes. Blood also contains all of the food substances and chemicals needed by the cell.

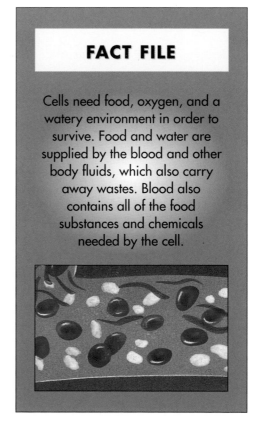

WHEN DO CELLS DIE?

All living things, plant and animal alike, are made from cells. An individual body cell is too small to be seen by the naked eye. Cells have a fixed life span and are replaced automatically as they die off. The more active the cell, the shorter its life.

Some white blood cells live for a very short time, and some types that consume dead cells and bacteria survive for only about 30 hours.

White cells that fight disease live for two to four years. Cells lining the intestine live for about five days before being replaced.

The life span of certain types of cells follows:

- Skin cells live for 19 days
- Sperm live for 2 months
- Eyelashes live for 3 to 4 months
- Red blood cells live for 4 months
- Liver cells live for 8 months
- Scalp hairs live for 2 to 4 years
- Bone cells live for 15 to 25 years

FACT FILE

There are three types of nerve cells, each with a different function. Motor neurons control the way muscles work. Sensory neurons carry messages from sense organs. Connector neurons pass messages between different parts of the nervous system.

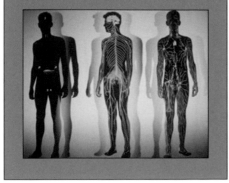

A human body cell

WHEN DOES THE BODY REPLACE DAMAGED CELLS?

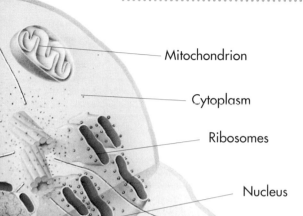

Mitochondrion

Cytoplasm

Ribosomes

Nucleus

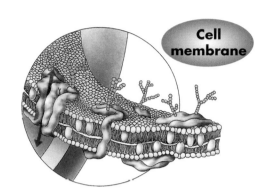

Cell membrane

Cells are able to divide very quickly to replace those that are old or that have died. Nerve cells are the only ones that cannot be replaced. Even nerve cells can sometimes grow new connections, however, if the message paths become damaged. Dead and dying cells are removed by white blood cells in the bloodstream, which actually eat them. The liver is also able to break down red blood cells, which are able to survive for only a short time. The cell's control area, the nucleus, contains all the information and instructions to keep the cells alive and functioning. The information the cell needs is in the form of immensely long coils of chemicals. These structures are known as *DNA*, which make up the genes.

FACT FILE

The largest cell in the human body is the egg cell, or ovum, which may be fertilized by a sperm cell and grow into a baby.

WHERE ARE OUR ADENOIDS?

Pharyngeal tonsil (adenoid)

The adenoids are located in the upper part of the throat, directly behind the nasal passages. Also known as the *pharyngeal tonsils*, they are a mass of gland-like tissue. A small amount of this tissue is always found in the throats of newborn babies. This normally shrinks until it disappears by the time the child is about10 years old. Occasionally this shrinking does not take place and the adenoid tissue increases to form a large growth. This growth is commonly known as "adenoids."

Consisting of lymphoid tissue, they form a continuous ring of this tissue around the back of the throat. When this tissue causes repeated infections in the throat, doctors remove it in an operation called an *adenoidectomy*.

FACT FILE

No one really knows the purpose of tonsils, but many medical scientists believe they aid in protecting the respiratory and digestive systems from infection. Tonsils consist of a type of tissue called *lymphoid* tissue. This tissue produces white blood cells, known as *lymphocytes*, that help fight infection.

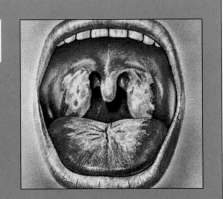

WHERE ARE OUR VOCAL CORDS?

Vocal cords are the main sound producers in human beings. These two small folds of tissue stretch across the larynx. Located between the back of the tongue and the trachea (windpipe), the larynx is part of the air passage in the throat. It is also known as the *voice box*, because it contains the vocal cords.

Muscles in the larynx stretch and relax the vocal cords. When we breathe, we relax our vocal cords so they form a *V*-shaped opening that lets air through. When we speak, we pull the vocal cords by the attached muscles, narrowing the opening. Then, as we drive air from the lungs through the larynx, the air vibrates the tightened vocal cords and sound results. The more the cords are stretched, the higher the sounds produced. The more relaxed the cords, the lower the sounds.

FACT FILE

The pitch of the voice is determined by the size of the larynx. Women's voices are usually pitched higher than men's because their vocal cords are shorter.

WHY IS WATER GOOD FOR US?

Water is an element that is essential for the existence of every form of life.

Over half of our bodies is made up of water, and this is true in varying degrees in other living creatures.

Human beings would die very quickly if they didn't drink water. This is because the cells that are the "building blocks" we are all made up of, have water molecules in them. Without water, cells would be very different and not support life as we know it.

During one day, a human being needs to ingest about two quarts of water as fluid as well as one quart in solid food. These foods are not really solid or dry but are made up of between thirty and ninety percent water. Examples are vegetables, fruit, bread, and meat.

Besides the water that comes into the body from outside, there are about ten quarts of water passing between the various organs within the body. Three quarts of the five quarts of blood in the vessels of our body is water, and this stays constant.

Cross-section of an animal cell

FACT FILE

Our sense of thirst is controlled in the brain. When the body requires more water, we experience the sensation of thirst. Usually our mouth and throat become dry—a signal for us to drink more fluids.

WHY ARE CELLS IMPORTANT?

Apart from water, the rest of the body is built from a large number of complicated chemicals. These chemicals, together with water, are assembled into our cells.

Each cell is self-contained and has a particular function in the body. There are more than 50,000 billion cells in the body. The shape and appearance of a cell depends on the type of job it has to do. Nerve cells are long and thread-like and can carry messages around the body along the nervous system.

Red blood cells are so tiny that they can be seen only under a microscope and are like flattened discs. The sole function of the blood cell is to combine with oxygen in the lungs and to exchange the oxygen for carbon dioxide in the tissues. White blood cells are shapeless so they can squeeze between other cells and attack invaders such as bacteria. Other cells control the production of essential substances called proteins.

FACT FILE

Metabolism is the term for all of the chemical activity that takes place inside the cells. Metabolism breaks down more complicated substances obtained from food. Our metabolic rate rises during vigorous exercise.

WHY DO PEOPLE GET ALLERGIES?

Many people have allergies to various things, from types of food (nuts for instance) and drugs to dust, pollen, plants, certain fabrics, bacteria, heat, sunlight, and even certain animals. This means they react in an extreme or unusual way to what are usually commonplace elements.

It's natural for the body to resist any foreign matter entering the tissues, producing antibodies to combine with it, making it harmless. But if it enters the body again, the antibodies tear themselves away from the body tissues to attack the substance. This produces the symptoms of an allergy by causing a chemical substance called *histamine* to be released.

FACT FILE

In spring and early summer, some people suffer from an allergic reaction to certain plants and pollens. This is called *hay fever* and can give the symptoms of a bad cold.

WHY DO SOME PEOPLE GET ASTHMA?

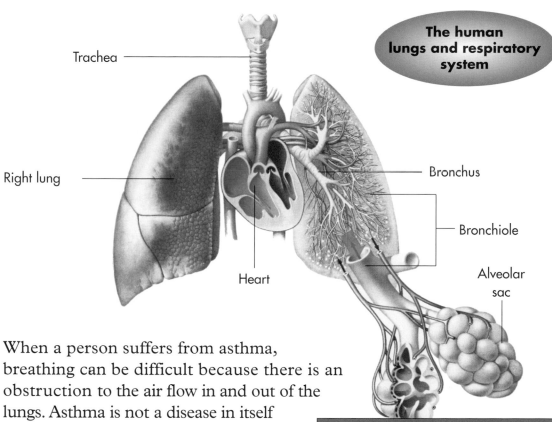

Trachea

Right lung

Heart

The human lungs and respiratory system

Bronchus

Bronchiole

Alveolar sac

When a person suffers from asthma, breathing can be difficult because there is an obstruction to the air flow in and out of the lungs. Asthma is not a disease in itself but is a symptom of some other condition. The cause of the problem can be an allergy, an emotional disturbance, or just atmospheric conditions. However, in young people under 30, an asthmatic condition is usually the result of an allergy. It might be a sensitivity to pollens, dust, animals, or certain foods or medicines.

Food allergies from eggs, milk, or wheat products are often the cause of asthma in children. People who suffer in this way are often put on special diets to avoid or minimize contact with these food products.

FACT FILE

People can develop allergies to many different foods. One of the most common is to dairy-related products.

WHY DO WE STOP GROWING?

Growing from an average length of about one foot, eight inches at birth, a human male triples this over the next twenty years and reaches an average height of about five feet, eight inches. But what stops us from just growing and growing?

Our body growth is controlled by a system of glands called the *endocrine glands*, which consist of the thyroid in the neck, the pituitary attached to the brain, the thymus which is in the chest, and the sex glands. The pituitary gland is the one that stimulates growth in our bones. If it functions too much our body and limbs grow too big. If it doesn't work enough, our growth is "stunted."

Our growth slows down by the age of 25, and we reach our maximum height at about the age of 35 or 40. After that, as the cartilages in our joints and spinal column dry up, we start to shrink about half an inch every ten years.

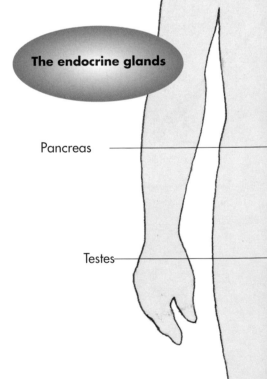

The endocrine glands

Pancreas

Testes

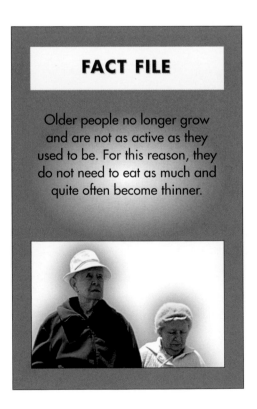

FACT FILE

Older people no longer grow and are not as active as they used to be. For this reason, they do not need to eat as much and quite often become thinner.

WHY DON'T WOMEN HAVE BEARDS?

Pituitary

Thyroid

Adrenals

Although it is often thought of as part of the bodies' "decoration," we must remember that hair on human beings had a more practical function than it does now. A newborn baby is covered with a fine down, which is replaced fairly quickly by the delicate hair we associate with all children. This is converted at the age of puberty into the final coat of hair which the person will have during adulthood.

The sex glands determine the development of hair in adults. The male sex hormone helps develop beard and body hair, while the growth of the hair on the head is slowed somewhat.

In contrast, the female hormone encourages the growth of hair on the head, while the growth of the beard and body hair is inhibited. Women do not have beards because their glands and hormones actively prevent it.

FACT FILE

The custom of shaving was introduced to England by the Saxons. Barbers first appeared in Roman times in 300 B.C. Today, there are a great variety of facial hair styles from beards and mustaches to the clean-shaven look.

FACT FILE

Vitamin C is an essential vitamin that helps to fight off infections and illnesses. This can be found naturally in oranges and other fruit and vegetables. It is very important that we include plenty of these in our everyday diet.

WHY DOES OUR TEMPERATURE RISE WHEN WE'RE ILL?

The average temperature of a healthy body is 98.6 degrees Fahrenheit. This temperature can rise with certain diseases, resulting in higher temperature, called *fever*.

One of the first things a doctor does when a person does not feel well is take his or her temperature with a thermometer, in order to find out whether the person has a fever.

Perhaps surprisingly, fever helps us fight off sickness by making the processes and organs in the body work faster. The body then produces more hormones, enzymes, and blood cells. The hormones and enzymes have to work harder when we are ill to perform their cleansing work. We get rid of wastes and poisons in our system as our blood circulates faster, and we breathe faster. It is important to get rid of fever as soon as possible because it destroys vital protein in our bodies.

WHY IS THE BODY WARM?

The energy that the body needs to perform all its various functions is produced by a process known as *combustion*, and the fuel for this combustion is the food we eat. This combustion is not an actual fire or extreme heat but a precise temperature, regulated by body substances that combine oxygen with the fuel in an orderly manner.

Like many such controls, the body maintains an average temperature, regardless of what is going on outside, from a center in the brain. Known as the temperature center, it consists of three parts: a control which regulates the temperature of the blood, a second that raises the temperature of the blood when it drops, and a third that cools it down when the temperature is too high.

We might not realize it, but when we shiver in the cold it actually produces heat. It is the body's reaction to the temperature of our blood dropping too low.

WHY DO WE TAKE ANTIBIOTICS?

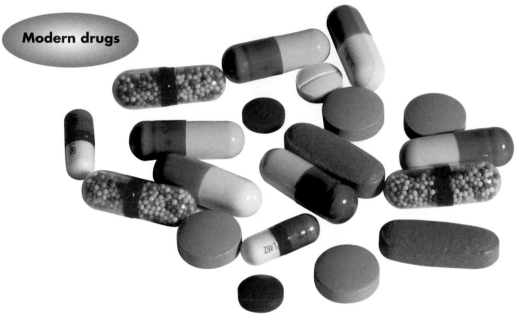

Modern drugs

There are certain chemicals that, when put into our bodies, stop the growth of various kinds of germs and help it to prevent disease. These chemicals are called *antibiotics*.

Microbes, for instance bacteria and molds, are tiny living things that can produce chemicals which wage war on the microbes of disease. These are used to make many antibiotics.

Antibiotics can be made to work in a variety of ways, and one antibiotic might act in different ways against different germs. In some cases, it might kill a germ, in another weaken it and let the body's natural defense mechanisms do the rest.

FACT FILE

Today, a lot of people are turning to natural remedies rather than prescribed drugs. These are made from natural products like roots, plants, flowers, and trees.

HOW ARE VIRUSES DIFFERENT FROM BACTERIA?

FACT FILE

Not all bacteria are harmful or cause disease. Our bodies contain millions of bacteria to break down dead and waste materials. Bacteria in the digestive sytem aid the digestive process.

Bacteria and viruses are the most significant causes of disease. Bacteria are simple plant-like organisms that can divide quickly. They cause many infections, such as boils and acne.

Viruses are much smaller and technically are not alive at all. They can take over the functioning of an infected cell and turn it into a factory producing millions more viruses. Viruses are responsible for many common diseases, such as colds and influenza.

The diagram below shows how a virus invades a cell: (1) they shed their outer layer (2) and take over the genetic material in the host cell in order to reproduce themselves (3). They begin to construct protein coats around the new viruses (4) and eventually burst out of the host cell (5) to leave it in an envelope (6) ready to infect new cells.

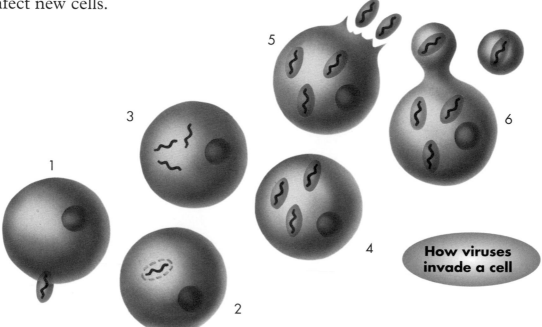

How viruses invade a cell

187

WHAT IS IMMUNITY?

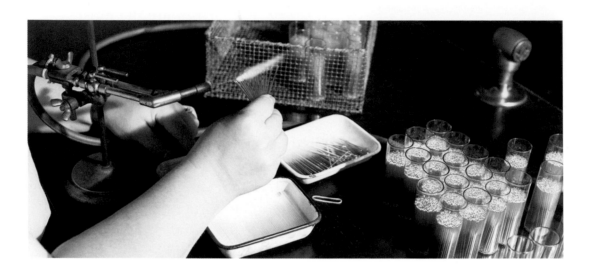

Our autoimmune system allows our body to recognize some viruses and bacteria that have already been in our body. This allows us to avoid getting ill with the same disease a second time. Some examples of illnesses that we can acquire immunity to are the childhood infections of measles, chicken pox, and rubella.

The first disease for which a vaccination was developed was smallpox. A British physician, Edward Jenner (1749–1823), noticed that milkmaids who had been infected with cowpox never got the more serious disease of smallpox. He deliberately exposed himself to cowpox and then to smallpox. He realized that his assumption had been correct. Today, vaccinations are available for diseases, such as measles, mumps, polio, cholera, typhoid, and yellow fever.

FACT FILE

The last naturally occurring case of smallpox was reported in Somalia in 1997. The general public is no longer routinely vaccinated against this disease.

WHY CAN'T WE CURE THE COMMON COLD?

Currently, there is no cure for diseases such as the common cold. There is not even a vaccine against any of the many forms of the virus that cause it. This is because the virus mutates very rapidly. Our immune system is not able to recognize a new form as it is being encountered. It is also impossible for scientists to develop vaccines to counter one form of the virus before another one has developed.

Vaccines against influenza do help to prevent epidemics. But this depends on scientists predicting in advance which forms of the virus are more likely to emerge and then preparing enough suitable vaccines for it. For example, if one particular form of influenza occurred widely last winter, it is less likely to occur this year. But if a form of the virus has not been seen for 20 years, few people will be immune to it and so they will choose to include that type of virus in this year's vaccine.

FACT FILE

Antibiotics cannot cure viral diseases, such as influenza. The overuse of antibiotics is one of the causes of the emergence of antibiotic-resistant forms of tuberculosis and MRSA.

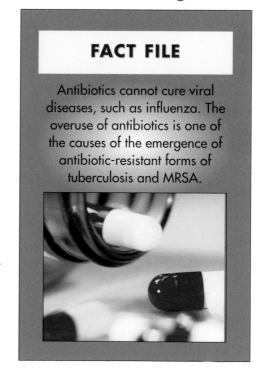

WHAT MAKES PEOPLE LAUGH?

Like many aspects of human behavior, laughter is not something we can explain easily. Even the most complex explanations are still only theories.

What we do know is that laughter can express a number of different feelings, and it is unique to human beings. It is difficult to decide what really makes people laugh, because each individual person will find a different thing funny.

As pure physical activity, laughter is good for us. It is good exercise for the lungs and an outlet for excess energy. Although no one really knows what makes people laugh or what the purpose of laughter is, it is a very good medicine and makes us feel better.

FACT FILE

When we smile we use 17 different muscles. When we frown we use 43 different muscles. So it is much easier to smile and laugh than to frown and be miserable. Did you know that the tongue is the strongest muscle in the body?

WHERE WAS THE FIRST ANESTHETIC USED?

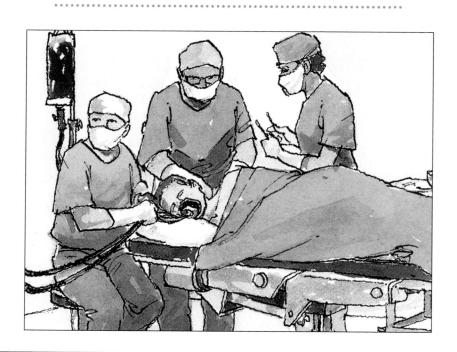

FACT FILE

With its pliers and saw, this box looks much like a tool box. In fact, it was a surgeon's case used during the Civil War.

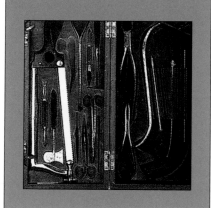

For thousands of years, physicians tried to dull pain during surgery by administering alcoholic drinks, opium, and various other drugs. But no drug had proved really effective in reducing the pain and shock of operations. Then in the 1840s, two Americans–Crawford Long and William T. G. Morton–discovered that ether gas could safely put patients to sleep during surgery. Long, a physician, and Morton, a dentist, appeared to have made the discovery independently. With an anesthetic, doctors could perform many operations that they could not attempt if the patient were conscious.

WHAT WAS THE FIRST PAINKILLER?

At least 3,500 year ago, the ancient Egyptians used a willow leaf mixture for pain relief. It is thought to have also been used widely as a folk remedy in Europe, Asia, North America, and Africa. In the 5th century B.C., Greek physician Hippocrates recommended that women chew on willow leaves or drink an extract of willow bark for pain relief during childbirth. Chinese records show that willow was widely used for pain relief there at the same time.

During the 19th century, various chemists tried to extract the active ingredient in willow. The first version, salicylic acid, was effective but caused stomach problems and nausea. In 1897, a group of German chemists obtained the first pure acetylsalicylic acid, which did not have the same side effects. Two years later, their compound went on sale as Aspirin.

FACT FILE

Prehistoric people probably also discovered that many plants could be used as drugs. For example, the use of quinine was used to prevent an illness called *malaria*. It is made from the bark of the cinchona tree.

HOW MUCH ENERGY DO WE NEED?

Nutrition is another word for the science of food and how the body deals with it. Like all living organisms, we need food to live. It provides the energy for everything we do, whether it is physical, mental, or emotional. It also supplies the chemicals and substances that our body's complex systems need to actually function.

The body's need for energy from diet varies not only with activity, sex, disease, and climate but also with age. The size of the figures in the diagram above show the comparative energy requirements from birth to adulthood. Up to two years old, the rapidly growing child needs more energy from diet than anyone in proportion to size. By old age, when metabolism is slowest, the need is far less.

FACT FILE

Proteins provide some energy, but more importantly, proteins serve as one of the main building materials of the body.

WHAT IS MRI?

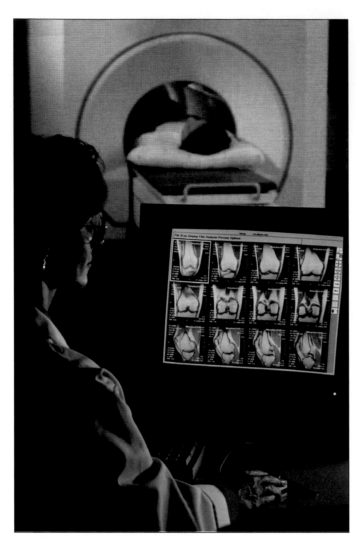

MRI, or *magnetic resonance imaging*, is a technique used by doctors in order to diagnose certain diseases, disorders, and injuries, by producing on-screen images of the tissues inside the body.

It is invaluable in that it allows doctors to examine the body for abnormal tissue without conducting actual surgery, nor does it expose patients to the kind of radiation we associate with Xrays.

One restriction on its use, however, is with people who have metal implants like artificial joints or heart pacemakers because the MRI uses a powerful magnet.

FACT FILE

An exciting area of medicine is the Human Genome Project. Its aim is to discover all of the 100,000 genes in the human body by studying DNA. This project involves the cooperation of eighteen different countries.

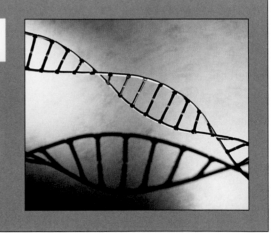

WHY DO WE PERSPIRE?

One of the ways we keep our body at the comfortable temperature of 98.6 degrees Fahrenheit is by perspiring. Perspiration washes out our body from within. Vessels in the skin open when we get too hot so that the extra heat can radiate away and help our perspiration evaporate. The fluid leaves the skin through millions of tiny openings in the form of microscopic drops, which evaporate quickly and cool the body when necessary.

FACT FILE

Perspiration is the body's own way of cooling down quickly. When a liquid evaporates, it takes heat from wherever it is located.

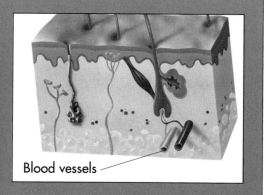

Blood vessels

ANIMAL

PHYSIOLOGY

CONTENTS

· · · · · · · · · · · · · · · ·

WHY DOES A CAMEL HAVE A HUMP? 198
WHAT ARE PARASITES? 199

WHY ARE SPIDERS NOT INSECTS? 200
WHY ARE SOME INSECTS BRIGHTLY COLORED? 201

WHY ARE SOME FROGS POISONOUS? 202
WHY DO FROGS DISAPPEAR IN WINTER? 203

WHY CAN'T FISH SURVIVE OUTSIDE WATER? 204
WHY IS BIRDS' VISION SO GOOD? 205

WHY DON'T SNAKES HAVE LEGS? 206
ARE CROCODILES THE SAME AS ALLIGATORS? 207

WHY DOES A GIRAFFE HAVE A LONG NECK? 208
WHY DOES A COW CHEW ITS CUD? 209

WHAT IS THE NEAREST LIVING RELATIVE TO MAN? 210
WHY ARE MONKEYS DIFFERENT FROM OTHER PRIMATES? 211

WHERE DOES THE KING PENGUIN PROTECT ITS EGGS? 212
WHERE IS A CLAM'S FOOT? 213

WHAT IS A CONTOUR FEATHER? 214
WHERE ARE AN OWL'S HORNS? 215

WHERE DOES A HEDGEHOG GO IN WINTER? 216
DOES A STARFISH HAVE EYES? 217

WHAT IS THE DIFFERENCE BETWEEN RABBITS AND HARES? 218
HOW IS AN OTTER ADAPTED FOR DIVING UNDERWATER? 219

WHY DO DEER SHED THEIR ANTLERS? 220
HOW DO WHALES BREATHE? 221

IS THE CHIMPANZEE A MONKEY? 222
HOW DOES A CHAMELEON CHANGE ITS APPEARANCE? 223

WHY DOES A CAMEL HAVE A HUMP?

The camel is called "the ship of the desert" and there is a good reason for it. Just as a ship is constructed to deal with all the problems that arise from being in the water, so a camel is built to live, travel, and survive in the desert. Where other animals would die from lack of food and water, the camel gets along very well. It carries its food and water with it. A camel prepares for a journey by doing nothing but eating and drinking for days, so much in fact that a hump develops on its back weighing as much as 100 pounds. The camel's hump, then, is a storage place for fat, which the camel's body will use up during the journey. The camel also has flask-shaped bags which line the walls of its stomach, and this is where it stores water. With such provisions, a camel is able to travel several days between water holes without drinking.

FACT FILE

There are two main kinds of camels: the Arabian camel, also called *dromedary*, which has one hump, and (2) the Bactrian camel, which has two humps.

WHAT ARE PARASITES?

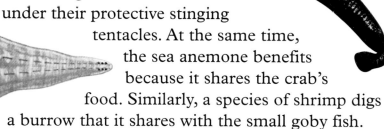

Parasites are animals that live at the expense of other animals. They rob the host animal of food and often cause it to become sick. However, in other types of relationships, different animals can help one another. This is called *symbiosis*. Some hermit crabs place sea anemones on their shells, hiding under their protective stinging tentacles. At the same time, the sea anemone benefits because it shares the crab's food. Similarly, a species of shrimp digs a burrow that it shares with the small goby fish. The fish benefits from being able to hide in the burrow while acting as a lookout to warn the shrimp of approaching predators.

Most true parasites are very simple animals, because they do not need complicated organs to digest their food. Some parasites are simply a mass of reproductive organs.

Different types of leech

FACT FILE

The fish leech can often be found on sticklebacks. It attaches itself to the body with its suckers. The mouth is found in the head sucker. A sharp proboscis is used to pierce soft areas such as the gills and the base of fins.

WHY ARE SPIDERS NOT INSECTS?

Spiders belong to the class of arachnids that also includes scorpions, ticks, and mites. None of these are classified as insects. Unlike insects, they have eight legs, eight eyes in most cases, no wings, and only two, not three parts to their bodies.

Spiders are found in practically every kind of climate. They can run on the ground, climb plants, run on water, and some even live in water.

The spider manufactures a silk, which it uses to spin its web, in certain glands found in its abdomen, or belly. At the tip of the abdomen there are spinning organs that contain many tiny holes. The silk is forced through these tiny holes. When the silk comes out, it is a liquid. As soon as it comes in contact with the air, it becomes solid. Spiders are meat-eaters, feeding on insects and other spiders which they trap in their webs.

FACT FILE

The scorpion is related to the spider. A scorpion has four pairs of walking legs and a pair of strong pincers that it uses to grasp its prey. It also has a long, thin, jointed tail that ends in a curved, pointed stinger. This stinger is connected to poison glands.

WHY ARE SOME INSECTS BRIGHTLY COLORED?

Insects try to protect themselves from their enemies in many different ways. Some insects, such as wasps and ants, have powerful stingers or are able to shower their attackers with poisonous fluid. The hoverfly does not sting, but its coloring is so much like a wasp or bee's that enemies are wary of it. Other insects, such as a walking stick, use camouflage. They look like the leaves and twigs where they feed. The bright coloring on some insects warns its enemies that it may be poisonous.

FACT FILE

The ladybug is a brightly colored insect. The ladybug is a very useful insect in the garden because it eats aphids, which eat the plants and flowers.

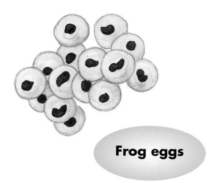

Frog eggs

The internal organs
of a frog are typical of
vertebrate animals,
although their lungs and
heart are much simpler
than those of mammals
and birds.

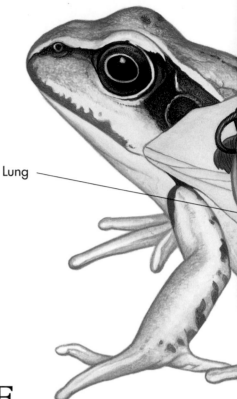

Lung

WHY ARE SOME FROGS POISONOUS?

Not all frogs are poisonous, but
some have developed a venom that
they can use if they come under
attack from predators. The common
toad contains a poison that it exudes
through its skin, if attacked. Dogs
and cats commonly experience this
poison, but they seldom suffer
serious effects. It does teach them,
though, to avoid these amphibians.
Cane toads are very large toads that
contain a drug capable of causing
hallucinations if they are eaten. The
skin of some frogs and toads contain
some of the most powerful poisons
known to human beings.

FACT FILE

The South American arrow frog
is extremely poisonous. It
announces this danger by being
very brightly colored.

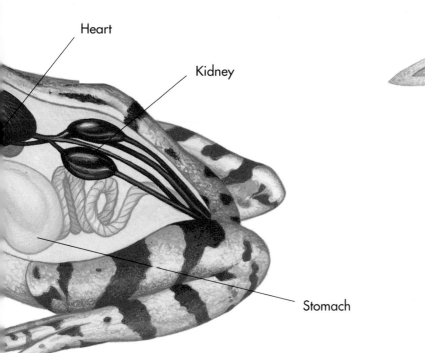

Heart

Kidney

Stomach

A tadpole

WHY DO FROGS DISAPPEAR IN WINTER?

FACT FILE

A frog's eyes are positioned on the top of its head so that it can see above the water's surface. In this way, it can always be on the alert for predators.

Frogs can vary a lot in color, shape, and size. Among the smallest are the inch-long tree frogs found in the United States, compared to the bullfrog, which can be up to eight inches long, with legs ten inches in length.

Where do the frogs go in the winter? In the northern climates, as the weather gets colder, some frogs immerse themselves in the mud of a pond and stay there until spring. Because ponds do not freeze solid even in the coldest winters, the frog is safe from the elements.

WHY CAN'T FISH SURVIVE OUTSIDE WATER?

Fish are specially adapted so that they can breathe underwater. They have special organs called *gills*. Gills are bars of tissue at each side of the fish's head. They carry masses of finger-like projections that contain tiny blood vessels. The fish gulp in water through their mouths and pass it out through their gills. The gills are rich in blood, and they extract oxygen from the water and pass it into the fish's blood.

In this way, the gills have the same function as the lungs of air-breathing animals. But gills would not work without water.

FACT FILE

Most of a fish's body is composed of powerful muscles. Its internal organs are squeezed into a tiny area. The fins are used to propel and stabilize the fish in the water.

WHY IS BIRDS' VISION SO GOOD?

Vision is the dominant sense of nearly all birds. In most birds, the eyes are placed so far to the side of the head that they have mainly monocular vision, meaning that each eye scans a separate area. This feature is shared by all hunted creatures who depend on vision to warn them of possible danger. Birds of prey and owls have eyes set more to the front of the head, offering a wider angle of binocular vision, which is vitally important for judging distance. Birds also have a third eyelid which moves sideways across the cornea and keeps it moist, without interrupting their vision.

FACT FILE

Accuracy is crucial for a hunting bird like the eagle, which relies on its keen eyesight, first to spot the prey and then to catch it. The eagle's eyes are positioned sufficiently far forwards to give it binocular, or three-dimensional vision.

WHY DON'T SNAKES HAVE LEGS?

Although snakes have evolved, as we now know them, without legs, they probably did have them at some stage in their development. One theory is that they evolved from types of burrowing lizards whose legs disappeared altogether over time. Although they have no legs, they are very mobile nonetheless. One contributing factor is the belly scales that usually cover the whole undersurface of a snake. Snakes move in different ways. One is the concertina method, which is used in climbing and sidewinding, where a loop of the body is thrown to one side. There is also the lateral undulatory movement, where the sanke's body forms *S*-shaped curves. Finally, there is the rectilinear movement, where the snake uses its scales.

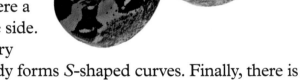

FACT FILE

Lizards and snakes belong to the highest order of reptiles. The main difference between lizards and snakes is in the structure of the jaws. In snakes, both upper and lower jaws have movable halves with sharp teeth.

ARE CROCODILES THE SAME AS ALLIGATORS?

Both crocodiles and alligators spend most of their lives in swamps and rivers in warm climates, although they breathe air through nostrils on the top of their snouts. They close these nostrils when they dive below the water. Caymans and gavials are relatives of crocodiles and alligators.

One way of telling them apart is that crocodiles show the fourth tooth in their lower jaw when their mouths are closed. Alligators, on the other hand, do not. It is probably wise not to go near enough to a live crocodile to find out, however, as they have been known to attack humans.

FACT FILE

The Komodo dragon is a huge monitor lizard found living in Indonesia. This fearsome lizard is known to live for about 100 years. It can grow to a length of more than 100 inches (3 meters).

An alligator

A crocodile

WHY DOES A GIRAFFE HAVE A LONG NECK?

Giraffes in the wild

FACT FILE

The elephant is also an unusual animal because of its very long trunk. It is an extension of the nose and upper lip and serves the elephant as hand, arm, nose and lips all at once.

The tallest of all living animals, the shape and size of the giraffe is tailor-made for it to obtain its food. A tropical vegetarian, its height enables it to reach leaves on trees in areas where there is little grass.

Even its 18-inch (46 cm) tongue comes into play, as the giraffe uses it to skillfully pick the smallest leaves off thorny plants without being pricked. Its long upper lip is used to tears of whole bunches of leaves at once.

Because its legs are so long, a giraffe can only eat or drink from ground level if it takes a peculiar position with its legs, spreading them out far enough to be able to reach down effectively.

WHY DOES A COW CHEW ITS CUD?

Thousands of years ago, certain animals that didn't have any protection against their predators, adapted their ways of eating that allowed them to feed themselves and survive attack at the same time. This meant that they had to gobble food and swallow it quickly without chewing it, so they could run from their foes. After finding a safe refuge, they could then chew their food leisurely. Some present-day animals, such as cows, still eat in this manner. It is called *chewing the cud* and the animals are called *ruminants*. This way of eating is possible because these animals have complicated stomachs with five compartments. Each of these compartments processes the food.

WHAT IS THE NEAREST LIVING RELATIVE TO MAN?

The great apes are the nearest living relative to man. There are four species of great ape: the orangutan, chimpanzee, gorilla, and the gibbon. Chimpanzees are particularly smart and are one of the few animals to actually use tools. Apes generally walk on all fours but are able to stand and walk on two feet just like human beings. Apes also have fingers and thumbs like a human hand, which makes them able to pick up and hold things as we do. The hair on an ape's head also turns gray with age just as with human beings. Baby gorillas, like human being babies, learn to crawl at about ten weeks and walk at about eight months old.

FACT FILE

Apes like this gibbon give birth to helpless young that need to be watched for a long time. Apes can look after their young for as long as five years.

WHY ARE MONKEYS DIFFERENT FROM OTHER PRIMATES?

All monkeys are primates. It is easy to tell them apart from people and apes because they have tails. Their tails, which are generally long, can be used as an extra arm or leg to cling onto branches. A spider monkey, from South America, can actually hang by its strong tail, leaving both hands free for feeding. They live in family groups and spend much of their time in trees. They are careful as they leap from one tree to another as there could be danger close by. A large eagle might swoop from above or a leopard could be lurking below so they have to be careful not to lose their footing.

FACT FILE

Monkeys have a varied diet. They eat a wide variety of food, from flowers, leaves, and fruit, to insects and small frogs.

WHERE DOES THE KING PENGUIN PROTECT ITS EGGS?

King penguin

King penguins do not build nests but tuck their single egg under their bellies while resting it on their feet. It is protected there by a large fold of skin. The mother and father penguin take turns keeping the egg warm in the cold.

Because the king penguin's main concern is to maintain a constant body temperature, they are restricted to areas that do not have temperature fluctuations. Their territories can be rocky, icy, or snowy, as long as there is water with an abundance of food available. Colonies can be as large as 10,000 penguins, and each bird keeps its distance from one another. In these close quarters, coming too close can result in a nasty jab or flipper slap! The king penguin, second in size only to the large emperor penguin, is one of the biggest birds around, up to 3 feet in height (0.914 m). They can swim at speeds of 6 mph, and use their wings as flippers to fly through the water, and then hop out onto the rocky shore. Unlike many other penguins, the king penguin runs with its feet and doesn't hop while on land.

FACT FILE

Baby chicks are born from their greenish-white eggs nearly naked, but quickly become covered in a brown woolly fuzz to keep them warm. The adult penguins are often dwarfed by their chicks.

WHERE IS A CLAM'S FOOT?

FACT FILE

The giant clam lives on coral reefs in the Red Sea, the Indian Ocean, and the western Pacific. These clams can grow to a length of more than 4 feet (1.2 m).

Clams are a type of mollusk, soft-bodied animals that have no bones. Clams burrow in the mud or sand with a large muscular organ called a *foot*. The foot spreads beneath the body, and its muscles move in a rippling motion that makes the animal move forward. A protective shell covers the soft body of the clam. They are found on the floor or shores of oceans, streams, and lakes around the world. Clams also have a heart, blood vessels, and kidneys. Clams feed on tiny water organisms called *plankton* or on small, shrimp-like animals.

WHAT IS A CONTOUR FEATHER?

Jay

Birds have two kinds of feathers, contour and down. Feathers are the light, thin growths that cover a bird's body and contour feathers are found in special areas of the bird's body called *pterylae*. From the pterylae, the relatively big contour feathers cover the bird, almost completely like a fan. Down feathers, on the other hand, are found all over the bird's body. Feathers consist chiefly of a substance called *keratin*, which also is part of the hair on mammals and scales of fish and reptiles. But feathers have a unique and complicated branching pattern.

Parts can vary greatly on a feather. Feathers enable a bird to fly and help it maintain a constant body temperature. Like most body coverings, though, feathers gradually wear out. Birds shed them and grow a new set at least once a year in a process known as *molting*.

FACT FILE

For thousands of years, human beings have used feathers in many ways. Ancient cultures used feathers for anything from arrows to headdresses. Until the 19th century, most people wrote with quills made from feathers. Today, feathers are still used extensively in upholstery and pillows.

WHERE ARE AN OWL'S HORNS?

Owls are characterized by short, broad bodies, hooked beaks, and strong feet with sharp talons. Most have tufts of feathers on their heads called "ears" or "horns." An owl's plumage is usually a bland color that matches its surroundings, and the fluffy feathers make it appear larger than it is.

Nocturnal, the owl has been nicknamed the "night watchman" of our yards because it hunts for prey at night, ridding us of pests such as rodents. There are more than 145 species of owl all over the world, in every type of climate.

FACT FILE

The eyes of most owls are directed forward. For this reason, owls can watch an object with both eyes at the same time. Owls cannot move their eyes in their sockets so they must move their heads to watch a moving object.

WHERE DOES A HEDGEHOG GO IN WINTER?

The hedgehog is a small animal with short ears and legs, and a short tail and a long nose. It looks quite similar to a porcupine. It has stiff, needle-like growths, called *spines*, all over its back to protect it from its enemies. When it is in danger, the hedgehog rolls itself into a spiny ball.

In winter, a hedgehog goes into hibernation, which is a sleep-like state. They hibernate to protect themselves against the cold and reduce their need for food. During hibernation, the hedgehog's body temperature becomes lower than normal and its heartbeat and breathing slow down greatly. An animal in this state needs little energy to stay alive and can live off fat stored in its body.

FACT FILE

A hedgehog may have two litters between May and August. They have around five young, which open their eyes at two weeks. They can roll up beginning at 11 days and are weaned by the time they are six weeks old.

DOES A STARFISH HAVE EYES?

Most species of starfish, spiny-skinned animals, live in all of the world's oceans. They have five thick arm-like extensions and look somewhat like five-pointed stars. Some species have as many as 40 arms. The starfish body has a central disk and arms. There is a mouth on the underside of the central disk which leads straight into the stomach. On the outside, a groove extends from the mouth to the tip of each arm, with rows of slender tube feet. These feet often have suction disks on their ends, lining these grooves. It uses the tube feet for crawling and obtaining food. The starfish, which does not have a brain, has nerve cords suspended in the grooves of its arms. It senses light with a small eye at the tip of each arm.

FACT FILE

Many starfish can drop off arms as a defensive reaction. They can then grow new arms to replace the old ones.

IS THE CHIMPANZEE A MONKEY?

Chimpanzees are a kind of African ape. They are the most intellegent of all monkeys. They are playful and easy to train. They are also related to gorillas, orangutans, and gibbons.

The chimpanzee lives in tropical Africa from Lake Victoria in the east to Gambia in the west. The species is divided up into three subspecies: the central chimpanzee, the eastern or long-haired chimpanzee, and the western chimpanzee.

FACT FILE

The gibbon is becoming endangered. Their forest homes are being destroyed. The capture of young animals for food or for sale as pets threaten these species with extinction.

HOW DOES A CHAMELEON CHANGE ITS APPEARANCE?

The chameleon is a species of lizard. There are around 85 species, and most live in the forests of Africa and Madagascar.

The chameleon, which may be green, yellow, or white one minute and brown or black the next is known for its ability to change its appearance. There are many other kinds of lizards that also have this characteristic. A chameleon may also become spotted or blotched. Many people believe chameleons change to blend with their environment, but the changes actually occur in response to changes in light or temperature, or as the result of fright or some other reaction to outside events. The chameleon's appearance is regulated by body chemicals called *hormones*, affecting the pigments in their skin.

FACT FILE

Chameleons that live in trees have a long, sticky tongue with which they capture prey. The tongue, which may be as long as their entire body, is controlled by powerful muscles in the throat. It shoots out so rapidly that the human eye can hardly see it.

PICTURE ACKNOWLEDGMENTS

Corbis UK Ltd. / 173 top, 192 / David Aubrey 189 bottom / Lester V. Bergman 172 bottom / Bettman 188 top, 188 bottom / Mark L. Stephenson 69 top / Tom Stewart 172 top, 189 top